First published in 2008 by Pocket Essentials
P.O.Box 394, Harpenden, Herts, AL5 1XJ
www.pocketessentials.com

Editor: Nick Rennison
Indexer: Richard Howard

A CIP catalogue record for this book is available from the British Library.

ISBN 978-1-84243-243-3

2 4 6 8 10 9 7 5 3 1

Typeset by Avocet Typeset, Chilton, Aylesbury, Bucks
Printed and bound in Great Britain by J. H. Haynes & Co. Ltd., Sparkford

Contents

CONTENTS

Introduction

At some point during the 1880s the teenage Mary MacDonald left her home on an island off the coast of County Donegal in the north west of Ireland to take up a position as a maid in a convent in Birmingham. It was more than 30 years after the worst of the Irish Famine, but times were still hard in the west of Ireland and emigration to find work and escape from poverty was a common occurrence. It must have been difficult at first for Mary to adjust to a life in an industrial city, not least because, when she arrived, she didn't speak any English. Her family, like the majority of the people from that part of Ireland at the time, were Irish speakers and English, if it was spoken at all, would only have been used when talking to outsiders. Although I don't know what conditions were like in the convent, it is easy to imagine the regime being strict and the work hard. At some point in her late teens or early twenties, Mary MacDonald left the convent and got married to a young man, who also came from within the Irish Catholic community in Birmingham, and they started a family.

There is nothing exceptional about this story, but it is important to me because Mary MacDonald was my great-grandmother. It is one part of the story of my family, of how they left Ireland and established themselves in Birmingham. I have never questioned this version of events and, in writing it down now, I have not checked to make sure I have got the story straight. Other members of my family may well tell it in a different way entirely, but this is my version, this is the way I remember it being told to me.

The story can be seen as one strand of my own personal foundation myth. It tells me something about where I am from and, to a certain extent, who I am. A fascination with our origins and ancestry appears to be a universal trait, shared throughout humanity and across all cultures, and, going back to the time before the invention of the written word, one of the ways of expressing, explaining and preserving these ideas was through storytelling. This, in essence, is what mythology is. Mythology uses stories to offer explanations for what might otherwise be inexplicable.

Another of my purposes in telling the story is to demonstrate my own Celtic roots. I am, in a rather obvious fashion, trying to give myself some connection to the subject matter of this book, as if, by doing so, I have a more legitimate claim on the stories than someone who cannot trace their ancestry back to the west coast of Ireland. This is, of course, complete nonsense, but it does illustrate that stories can have more meanings and purposes than they might initially appear to have. Myths certainly fall into this category. They can offer explanations to the big questions (life, the universe and everything, as Douglas Adams put it in *The Hitchhiker's Guide to the Galaxy*); they are a way of understanding the world in which we live; they can reinforce cultural ties by showing listeners their place within society;

and they can act as a resource of information. Although not often discussed in great detail in the academic literature on the subject, myths can also be enjoyable and entertaining. In fact, it could be argued, their primary function is to engage and enthral. We all love a good story, whether we get all its nuances and inferences or we are simply swept along by the narrative. It would be interesting to learn, for instance, how many of the fans of the Star Wars films, which are clearly based on traditional storytelling and have storylines involving heroes, princesses and tyrants and the fight between good and evil, could really care less about any deeper meanings the films may have. Most probably viewers watch them for their entertainment value alone.

This book is primarily concerned with the surviving mythology of the people of the Atlantic fringes of north west Europe, collectively known as the Celts: the Irish, Welsh, Scottish, Manx, Cornish and Bretons. It is a book of two halves. The first half begins by briefly considering myths in general, what they are and what they are for, before going on to tackle the controversial question of who the Ancient Celts, the people who inhabited Britain and Ireland before the Romans arrived, actually were and what the society in which they lived was like. Chapter three then deals with storytelling in general and how, and in what form, the mythic stories, generated as part of an oral tradition and in a pre-Christian culture, survived the transition to Christianity to come down to us in the modern age.

The vast majority of the surviving myths come from Ireland and, to a lesser extent, from Wales. Because of this, the second half of the book, which concerns the myths themselves, concentrates on these two countries. This is not intended to imply that the myths of the other Celtic regions were in any way inferior to those of Ireland and Wales and, in Chapter 6, consideration is given to these. Unfortunately, for the most part, the myths of Scotland and Man and of Cornwall and Brittany have been lost and their richness can now only be inferred from folktales, the telling of which among speakers of the Celtic languages continued until quite recently. In some respects, it continues today.

This, then, is a book about stories and storytelling, about the heroes Cúchulainn and Fionn mac Cumhaill and the heroines Deirdre and Rhiannon, about this world and the Otherworld. The stories can be tragic, romantic, intense or funny and, sometimes, they can be combinations of any and all of these. They can be magical or grimly realistic, epic in scale or highly personal, full of symbolism and allusion or entirely straightforward, brilliantly realised works of literature or, on occasion, contrived nonsense. The world was a very different place when these stories were being told by bards and storytellers and we will probably never fully understand all the hidden meanings and references they contain but, even so, they can have a relevance to the world in which we now live. Like all great art, the Celtic myths are fundamentally concerned with what it is like to be a human being and, whatever else changes, this is one thing that stays much the same.

On Mythology

The Purpose of Myth

Some of the greatest minds of the twentieth century – Sigmund Freud, Carl Gustav Jung, Vladimir Propp, Claude Levi-Strauss, to name but a few – have exercised their considerable intellects on the subject of mythology. Although it is beyond the scope of this book to consider the development of mythology as an academic discipline,[1] it is certainly worth exploring aspects of the general thought on the subject as a means both of introducing the specific field of Celtic Mythology and of placing it within an overall framework.

Perhaps the most obvious starting point is to define what is meant by the term myth and to consider what, if anything, differentiates myths from other similar forms of story such as legends or folktales. The main entry under myth in the *Shorter Oxford English Dictionary* gives a clear and uncluttered definition:

A traditional story, either wholly or partially fictitious, providing an explanation for or embodying a popular idea concerning some natural or social phenomenon or some religious belief or ritual; specifically one involving supernatural persons, actions, or events; a similar newly created story.[2]

This is the sense in which the word myth is used in this book. As the definition makes clear, myths are first and foremost traditional stories. A great deal has been written about the purpose of these stories but, for them to have survived and to have been passed down through generations of storytellers, the stories themselves must have engaged, informed and, above all else, entertained the audience. This aspect of myths has been much less remarked upon in the academic literature, perhaps because it is self-evident that a story which bores its audience will not be one that remains in any successful storyteller's repertoire for long.

Describing what a myth is, then, would appear to be quite straightforward, but a problem arises out of the modern usage of the word. A second definition in the dictionary states that a myth is a widely held story or belief which, on examination, turns out to be entirely untrue. An example could be the myth of the American dream, in which people in America, whatever their background or financial status, are supposed to have an equal chance of achieving whatever they set out to do through hard work and perseverance. As attractive as this idea may be, all of us know, if we are being honest, that it is no more true in America than it is anywhere else in the world.

When someone uses the phrase, 'It's a myth', what they are saying is that whatever they are referring to is untrue. It is easy to envisage the extension of this usage to include the stories that make up a mythology, giving rise to the idea that these stories are untrue and that the entire mythology constitutes a false way of thinking. But myths, of course, don't deal with the world they describe in terms of what is specifically true and false. In the same way, novels and films are not necessarily concerned directly with reality. Nobody, for example, would think to describe Tolstoy's *Anna Karenina* as untrue, although the situations and characters described were invented by the author. The purpose of the novel is not to give accurate biographies of real people but to examine the actions and motivations of the characters in order to cast some light on what we may call the human condition. Myths, like modern fiction or art in general, can be seen as a way of attempting to describe what may otherwise be inexplicable and to provide, at least to some extent, meaning and understanding amidst the complexities and vicissitudes of life.

A further problem arises through the tendency to confuse the stories making up a mythology with the otherwise separate subject of mysticism. Presumably this confusion occurs not only because both mythology and mysticism deal with the unknown and otherworldly, although in different ways, but also because the words look and sound similar. Mysticism deals with beliefs that transcend human understanding, including those of mainstream religions, although today the word is often associated with occult and alternative belief systems. An example of the confusion arising out of the conflation of these two words is the fact that many bookshops shelve books on mythology, including highbrow academic tomes on the subject, in sections with titles like 'New Age' or 'Mind, Body and Spirit' when, in many cases, these books would be much more suited to the literature sections.[3] It would be unthinkable to consider shelving *The Iliad* and *The Odyssey*, the bedrocks of the entire Western literary canon, anywhere other than under literature, although the only difference between these two works of epic poetry and many myths is that *The Iliad* and *The Odyssey* have a named author.

Celtic mythology has been viewed through the lens of mysticism to a greater degree than has been the case with the myths of any other culture. One of the reasons for this has been the tendency of neighbouring Anglo-Saxons to belittle the people of the Celtic fringes of the British Isles by characterising them as (amongst other things) overly superstitious, possessed of a weak-minded fascination with fairies and ghosts that compared unfavourably with their own sturdy, commonsensical belief in Anglican Christianity. The Celtic Revival, beginning in the eighteenth century, also emphasised the otherworldly, mystical aspects of Celtic culture to the point where it became almost impossible to consider anything to do with the Celts without getting misty-eyed and sentimental.

In the introduction to *A Celtic Miscellany*, Kenneth Jackson makes this point, saying, 'It has been the fashion to think of the Celtic mind as something mysterious, magical, filled with dark broodings over a mighty past.' He goes on to dismiss these ideas as preposterous and considers how they have informed our appreciation of the mythology, saying:

> In fact, the Celtic literatures are about as little given to mysticism or sentimentality as it is possible to be; their most outstanding characteristic is rather their astonishing power of imagination.[4]

While Kenneth Jackson's unequivocal language may be something of an overstatement, he is nevertheless making a valid point. The stories making up the mythology can be seen as one way of attempting to deal with a world full of uncertainty and imponderable questions. It does not necessarily follow that the people who listened to the stories gained any greater spiritual knowledge or were more in touch with higher spheres of consciousness than anyone else.

Myths may involve dealing with the esoteric up to a point but, taken overall, they are often much more down to earth. There is a huge literature on the purpose of myths within the cultures which generated them, much of which goes on to compare the similarities that have been uncovered between the myths of different cultures, giving rise to theories suggesting that there are universal aspects to these purposes, applicable to humanity in general. A detailed discussion of this subject would easily fill the rest of this book and many more volumes besides. What follows is a very brief summary.

As well as entertaining the audience, myths can be a way of passing on information from one generation to the next, in effect by acting as a store of knowledge. Stories are relatively easy to remember and can be retained through frequent retelling. In cultures where nothing is written down, which are where myths are generated, the art of remembering important information involves constantly repeating it, otherwise it will be forgotten. Once this has happened, there is no way of retrieving the lost information. It is not easy to envisage from the point of view of the 'Information Age' we now live in but, before the advent of writing, storytellers and the store of knowledge they carried with them acted as the collective memories of the societies in which they lived. They would have been as important in an oral culture as libraries, the media and the internet are now.

Some of the common features shared between different mythologies include those stories which tell of how the world was formed in the first place – the creation myths – and those telling how a group of people came together to form a society – the foundation myths – together with stories of how that society was maintained and enhanced through the deeds of heroic ancestors (a particular feature of Celtic mythology). These stories impart a sense of togetherness and belonging to the listeners, both through the shared experience of being part of a communal audience and by reinforcing the cultural identity of the group. By telling people where they came from and how they came to be together, the myths provide answers to some of the fundamental questions common to humanity, allowing individuals to find their place in the world and live within the framework of beliefs of their society.[5]

This is very much like the purpose of religion. Some commentators have suggested that religions are made up of an amalgamation of mythology and ritual, although this association is not usually much appreciated by the followers of different religions, probably because of the modern usage of the word myth to describe an idea that is not true. A further feature of mythology also shares common ground with religion. Myths provide examples of how to live correctly within a society and how to behave when confronted by difficult situations. In other words, the myths demonstrate a system of ethics and morals in much the same way as religions do. Many biblical stories, for example, could just as well be called myths if it were not for the modern usage of the word.

In summary then, myths present the people who listen to them with a way of looking at the world which is consistent across the society to which they belong. In an uncertain world, which does not often submit to rational explanations and where the threat of misfortune is ever present, the stories making up a mythology often offer answers to questions which would otherwise remain beyond the reach of human consciousness.

Mythos and Logos

One way of getting closer to an understanding of what is involved in mythology is to consider the duality between the ideas represented by the Ancient Greek words *mythos,* meaning 'story', and *logos*, which means 'reason' and is the root of the word logic.

The duality exists between two different, not necessarily opposing, ways of thinking about and explaining the world which are analogous to the difference between art and science. Art, it could be argued, makes use of the imagination in an attempt to describe what it is like to be a human being, while science seeks to explain the physical world through direct observation and the use of deductive reasoning. Since the Enlightenment of the seventeenth and eighteenth centuries – the Age of Reason as it is sometimes called – we have come to expect the phenomena of the world to be explained along rational scientific lines, in other words, to make use of *logos*. Previously, before scientific method was available, explanations had to be based more on the imagination, on *mythos*.

Mythology explains how the world works by telling stories of how it was created and how human beings came into existence, leading some commentators to describe it as the science of the ancient world. If mythology is considered in terms of providing scientific explanations, then it fails completely in its purpose and can be easily dismissed. But this is to think of myths in terms of *logos*, a concept to which they do not, in any sense, conform. Myths employ such literary techniques as symbolism, allegory and metaphor in an attempt to describe what it is like to live in the world and what it is like to be a human being rather than to describe directly how we experience the world.

If myths are thought of as science, they become entirely redundant, products of an age when the state of knowledge was insufficient for the purpose. But, if they are thought of as art, then they retain their relevance. In other words, myths are not the product of *logos* but, when taken for what they really are, they can be understood and appreciated, even in the modern age of supposed rationality.

Mythtime

One of the defining characteristics of myths is that the stories do not take place at any particular point in historical time, but at an unspecified point in the distant past, beyond the living memory of the people who are listening to the stories and at sufficient distance so they cannot recognise the protagonists of the stories as real historical figures. The placing of the story in what might be described as any time and no time, the mythtime, has been used to distinguish myths from legends. Legends, in contrast to myths, can be defined as stories occurring in specific historical periods and to characters who are thought of as having a historical reality.

Such clear distinctions are useful in a discussion of myths but, in reality, the lines between different categories are often much more blurred. The stories concerning King Arthur are, for example, generally described as legends, or sometimes as romances, although it is not known when the events related in the stories are supposed to have taken place or even if Arthur actually existed as a historical figure at all. In the past, it seems, storytellers didn't feel the need to classify their stories in the same way as we do now. This is particularly clear with the stories that constitute the subject of this book, many of which could equally well be called legends, sagas, epics or folktales. In academic circles they are often grouped together under titles which sound somewhat more highbrow, such as Early Irish Literature or the Literature of Medieval Wales but, in this book, for the sake of convenience and because the stories all take place at an unspecified time in the past, they are all lumped together under the one heading of Celtic Myths.

Stories occurring in mythtime, as opposed to a specified historical period, can often have a much broader appeal, as they are not limited to a particular audience. The storyteller is also allowed much greater flexibility to adapt the stories to the audience and to the circumstances contemporary to each performance. The stories were never set in stone, as stories are today, fixed in definitive printed versions. This can be illustrated by *The Odyssey*. Although the stories are set in the aftermath of the Trojan War, a conflict occurring in mythtime, the objects mentioned, such as the ships, weapons and clothing, can be dated to the seventh century BC, consistent with when, it is generally agreed, they were first written down. Rather than risk alienating the audience or go through the tedious process of explaining how people lived in the time in which the stories are set, the storyteller has simply updated and adapted them.

These characteristics – that the stories are not set in a particular period and that they are adaptable – are the result of their generation in oral cultures, before recorded history began. (This is a subject which will be expanded on in Chapter 3.) This has led to a theory that mythology was thought of in these oral cultures in the same way as history is today, as a record of what happened in the past. The problem with this theory is that it is really only a projection of how people from a written culture think of the past, as a progression of events leading up to the present, and does not reflect how people from an oral culture thought[6]. When there are no written records to consult to check the facts, the idea of the past and events which took place before living memory are very different.

In this sense then, mythology cannot be related to history. As Karen Armstrong says in her book *A Short History of Myth,* 'Mythology is an event which, in some sense, had happened once, but which also happened all the time'[7]. This idea, of myths representing stories of idealised events, corresponds with Jung's description of the characters in myths as being archetypes, the epitome of that character type, such as the best warrior and ultimate hero. These archetypal characters are, according to Jung, unconsciously recognised by large numbers of people who then have an expectation of how the characters will behave, an expectation fulfilled by the events of the story.

For a myth to persist in an oral culture, it has to continue to be told, otherwise it will be forgotten. It is those stories which strike a chord with their audience that will be the ones most likely to be retold, so those with the widest appeal, both because of the nature of the events related and because of audience identification with the characters, will be the ones to survive for the longest time and will be the ones most likely to get written down. A story occurring in mythtime has, for these reasons and because of its wider appeal, a better chance of surviving than a story set in historical time.

Armstrong goes on to say:

> Mythology is an art form that points beyond history to what is timeless in human existence, helping us to get beyond the chaotic flux of random events and glimpse the core of reality.[8]

It is, perhaps, this timeless quality which gives myths a dream-like quality and may also explain why Freud became so interested in them (particularly the Oedipus myth). The storylines of myths can also take on the appearance of coming straight out of dreams, with people and places apparently seamlessly merging into others and both people and animals shape-shifting, morphing from one physical form to another. This could be one of the reasons why myths share so much common ground across cultures, because they are, to some extent, the product of the unconscious mind, a part of the shared psychology of humanity or, as cognitive scientists might put it, a result of the hard-wiring of the brain.

Celtic Myth

So far this chapter has mostly dealt with what can be said about mythology in general, with the shared characteristics and themes occurring in myths across cultures, a subject sometimes referred to as Comparative Mythology. But this book is specifically about Celtic Myths, so, before moving on to consider the myths themselves, there are a few general points that should be made.

As already discussed, traditional stories often cross the boundaries between modern classifications of myth, legend and whatever other terms are being employed and this is particularly the case with Celtic myths. The Táin, for example, one of the longest of the surviving stories from Ireland, could just as well be described as epic literature as myth. Rather than getting pedantic about what constitutes a myth and what does not, and in the spirit of the storytellers, I don't propose to worry too much about the exact category of each story and consider all the extant stories under the heading of myth.

Much of Celtic mythology is concerned with the deeds of heroic ancestors, such as Cúchulainn and Fionn mac Cumhaill (sometimes written as Finn MacCool in English translations) from the Irish traditions. Although these heroes may possess great gifts, beyond what may be considered possible for any ordinary mortal, the stories in which they feature, unlike many myths from other cultures, rarely appear overtly concerned with the supernatural. There are a number of possible reasons for this, one of which is that traditional storytellers chose not take their stories into these supernatural realms. However, a closer reading of the stories actually reveals them to be intimately connected with the supernatural. It is just that these connections are not always immediately apparent. The surviving stories were first written down by scribes in the monasteries of early Christian Ireland, beginning in about the seventh century AD. It is impossible to know for certain but it is not hard to imagine these scribes either editing out any references to what they would have considered as pagan or only recording the stories which did not feature any of the gods and goddesses of pre-Christian Ireland in the first place. It is also possible that, by the time the stories were recorded, the storytellers who related the myths to the scribes, being Christians themselves, had adapted their stories to the needs of their society. However, if this had been the case, the surviving stories might be expected to exhibit more of a Christian slant than they actually do.

The majority of the surviving stories making up Celtic mythology come from the work of these monastic scribes in early Christian Ireland. A much smaller corpus of stories was also written down by scribes in Wales at a slightly later date, beginning in the thirteenth century. While the structure and content of these Welsh stories certainly reflect this late date, showing influences from the medieval styles of storytelling and from Arthurian romances, it is also apparent that the stories were based on a much earlier oral tradition in Wales.

The lack of any comparable written sources for the rest of the Celtic world is certainly frustrating but in some areas, particularly those more remote from the influence of English, where the Celtic languages continued to be spoken, aspects of the storytelling tradition itself survived into modern times. Traditional storytelling is a feature of an oral culture rather than a literate one and high levels of literacy today, together with the prevalence of mass media, have all but extinguished the tradition now. However, folklorists have for many years recorded the stories in a number of areas. This process began in the eighteenth century, when interest in the Celtic world in general was rekindled in what is known as the Celtic Revival. The authenticity of some of the folktales recorded in this way is very much open to doubt, but the writings of some of the more reliable folklorists are certainly worth considering, particularly as they often reveal the folktales to come from the same tradition as those myths recorded at a much earlier date.

The distinction between myths and folktales, like that between myths and legends, is something of an arbitrary one. For those regions where myths are lacking, but folktales have been recorded, some discussion of the latter will be included in this book, if for no other reason than that the folktales are all we have got.

The Celts

Introduction

As discussed in the previous chapter, common themes crop up in the mythologies of various different cultures, but the way these themes are expressed are generally much more specific to the particular culture within which they were generated. Myths, like everything else, do not exist in isolation and an appreciation of the specific cultures from which they come, in this case the so-called Celtic cultures of the Atlantic fringes of Western Europe, can only enhance an understanding of the mythologies.

This chapter takes a look at Celtic culture, particularly those facets of the culture pertinent to its mythology. But, before doing so, it is necessary to address the sometimes contentious issue of who the people we now generally call 'the Celts' actually were. The answer to this question may initially appear obvious. It is not difficult to define those described as Celtic in the modern world. The Celts are the inhabitants of Ireland and the western parts of the British Isles, namely Wales, Scotland, Cornwall and the Isle of Man, together with the inhabitants of Brittany, who think of themselves more as Breton than French. The common factor uniting these areas is a shared concept of national or regional identity based on the perception of being Celtic. This goes along with the persistence of the Celtic languages, even if they are not universally spoken and even if, as is the case in Cornwall and Man, they have had to be revived after becoming all but extinct.

While there can be no doubt about the connections between these regions, arguments have arisen in recent years about the use of the word Celtic to describe them. Opinions on this matter remain sharply divided, but the debate is worth considering, particularly when it throws new light on the subject of Celtic Mythology and when genetic studies carried out in Britain and Ireland over the past few years have shed new light on what it means to be a Celt today.

Who Were the Celts?

The answer to the question posed by the heading of this section appeared, at least up until quite recently, to have been firmly established in academic circles. It was based on the writings of classical authors, including Herodotus, Strabo and Pliny the Elder, the interpretation of linguistic studies of the Celtic languages, and the results of archaeological investigations of sites across Europe. It was thought that, during the European Iron Age and the classical period of the ascendancy of Greece and Rome, the Celts occupied a huge swath of Central Europe, between the Roman Empire and the Germanic tribes of the north, stretching from the Iberian Peninsular in the west right the way across to Anatolia, now part of Turkey, in the east.

In the fifth century BC, during the Iron Age, Celtic

tribes were thought to have invaded Britain and Ireland from continental Europe, displacing the previous inhabitants of the islands and bringing with them the cultural practices and artistic styles named after the sites where examples of these types of artefacts had first been found, at Halstatt in Austria and La Tène in Switzerland. The evidence for this was based on archaeological finds of artefacts, such as shields and swords, in sites across Europe, including in Britain and Ireland, which bore clear stylistic similarities to examples from Halstatt and La Tène. The two sites were considered to be the heartland of Celtic culture, which, it was thought, then spread out across Europe by migration and conquest.

The expansion of the Roman Empire through these Celtic lands, culminating in the invasion of Britain in AD 43, gradually led to the disintegration of Celtic culture as the process of Romanisation took place. Those areas of Britain not occupied by the Romans, including large parts of Wales and Scotland, together with the whole of Ireland, which was not subjected to a Roman invasion at all, maintained their Celtic cultures throughout this period. After almost 400 years, the Romans withdrew from Britain in about AD 410, leaving a power vacuum behind them which was filled by Germanic tribes – the Angles, Saxons and Jutes – who invaded from northern Europe.

Those parts of the British Isles which had been under Roman control were now subjugated by the invading Anglo-Saxons, while any remaining Celtic tribes were either annihilated or forced to move to the regions beyond the old borders of Roman territory. The Anglo-Saxon regions were thought to have been almost entirely cleansed of Celts and the people living there to have adopted a Germanic language, which would gradually evolve to become English.

Meanwhile the Celtic regions continued as they had before, maintaining their own culture and languages into the modern age. The Celtic languages spoken can be broadly divided into two linguistic groups, known as Goidelic, or Q-Celtic, which includes Irish, Scottish Gaelic and Manx, and Brythonic, and P-Celtic, consisting of Welsh, Cornish, Breton and the extinct Cumbric[9]. These are sometimes known as the Insular Celtic languages to distinguish then from the Celtic languages spoken on the European continent, such as Gaulish, Celtiberian and Lepontic, which are now all entirely extinct.

The above brief account can be considered as the standard version of Celtic history, prevalent in academic circles, promoted in popular books on the Celts and relatively uncontested until quite recently. A rising tide of unease began to develop during the 1990s among a group of archaeologists who didn't think that the archaeological evidence as it stood entirely fitted with this version of events. They began to examine the evidence more critically than it had been in the past and found that the whole edifice of Celtic history had been built on very shaky foundations. One of these archaeologists, Simon James, described the problem in uncompromising fashion:

It now seems that such archaeological 'cultures' [as the Celts] have been largely the products of the minds and expectations of archaeologists, rather than unambiguously observable realities: archaeologists have sought and emphasised similarity and uniformity, drawing boundaries where they did not necessarily exist.[10]

The use of the word 'Celts' to describe the Iron Age inhabitants of Britain and Ireland doesn't go back very much further than the beginning of the eighteenth century. It was used by the classical authors, in the sense of denoting 'others' or 'foreigners', to refer to the people to the north of Rome and what is now the south of France, but it was never used for those people living on the Atlantic fringes of Europe. Julius Caesar, for instance, made several expeditions to Britain, beginning in 55BC, during his campaigns in Gaul, but at no point did he describe the people he encountered there as related to the Celtic tribes he had conquered in Gaul[11].

In the early years of the eighteenth century, the distinguished Oxford antiquarian Edward Lhuyd recognised the similarities between the indigenous languages of the Atlantic coast and described them as belonging to the 'Celtic' group of languages, doing much to promote usage of the word 'Celt' in the process. Subsequent linguistic studies correctly linked these languages with Gaulish, Lepontic and Celtiberian and then reached the conclusion that, as the languages were similar, then the people throughout the regions where they were spoken must have all been the same people described by the classical authors as the Celts. As Professor Barry Cunliffe, one of the leading authorities on the Iron Age, has put it:

> To insist that the Celtic languages, called such by a
> seventeenth century antiquarian, represent Celts as

loosely defined by Greek and Roman writers involves a circular argument. The simple fact is that no classical writer ever referred to the inhabitants of Britain and Ireland as Celts[12].

The problem to which Cunliffe alluded has its roots in the assumption made by Lhuyd that the Celtic languages spread into Britain and Ireland from Brittany. Based on the evidence available in the eighteenth century, it was a perfectly reasonable conclusion to which to come but it is now generally held to be wrong. Linguistic studies have convincingly shown that the Breton language developed out of Cornish in about the fifth century AD. In other words, the movement of languages was from Britain to Brittany not the other way round. The linguistic evidence simply does not support the idea that the Celtic languages came into Britain through the movement of people from the European continent in the fifth century BC.

The circular argument to which Barry Cunliffe referred was then compounded by archaeologists in the nineteenth and twentieth centuries who interpreted finds of artefacts in terms of the movement of people into Britain and the displacement of the indigenous populations by these people. It was then a short step to envisage these new arrivals bringing the Celtic languages with them, thereby completing the circle of the argument. The critics of the standard version of Celtic history, not altogether surprisingly, see this as a process of interpreting the archaeology selectively in order to confirm a preformed idea, rather than allowing the evidence to speak for itself.

An unbiased review of the rapidly expanding evidence

from the Iron Age in Britain and Ireland finds very little support – some would say none at all – for a large scale invasion by Celts during the first millennium BC, or, in fact, during any other period. There is also no reason to suppose that the artistic styles generally described as being Celtic spread across Europe by any other method than acculturation, the exchange of such cultural features as language and artistic style when different cultures come into prolonged contact with each other. During the Iron Age, and going back thousands of years, extensive trade routes connected continental Europe with Britain and Ireland and this contact, it is now argued, resulted in the movement of artefacts bearing Celtic designs into the islands. These designs were taken up by the inhabitants of Britain in the same way as may now be seen with changing fashions in clothes and pop music. Barry Cunliffe suggests that the Celtic languages spread in a similar way to the artistic styles, becoming the common languages of trade along the routes of the movement of goods.

This line of argument leads to the conclusion neatly articulated by the archaeologist Francis Pryor, who is perhaps best known in Britain for his appearances on the TV programme *Time Team*:

> If there were no Iron Age invasions, then how did the Celts reach Britain? The answer can only be that they didn't come from outside. In other words, they were always here.[13]

This view expressed by Pryor is gradually coming to be accepted by the majority of archaeologists but, needless to say, the thorough debunking it gives to the standard version of the history of the Celts has proved controversial in wider society, particularly in those places where people think of themselves as being ethnically Celtic. There is no real reason why a reinterpretation of archaeological evidence, however radical its conclusions may be, should give such offence. The concepts of ethnicity and the nation state are both modern ones which have little relevance when projected back into British and Irish prehistory.

Celticity, as the idea of someone belonging to one of the Celtic regions is sometimes called, is a modern concept, dating back no further than the eighteenth century. This in no way undermines or devalues the cultural heritage of these regions which, in all probability, and as will be outlined in the following section, go back a great deal further than the fifth century BC. The connections between Celtic people, along with the many millions of people around the world who think of themselves as having roots in Celtic countries (the 'Celtic diaspora' as it is sometimes called) are as strong now as they have ever been. As Barry Cunliffe says:

> What is not in doubt, as anyone familiar with Galicia, Brittany, Ireland, or Wales will well know, is the very strong emotional appeal which the idea of sharing a common Celtic heritage has. Perhaps the only real definition of a Celt, now as in the past, is that a Celt is a person who believes him or herself to be Celtic[14].

These new trends in archaeology, then, do not affect the modern conception of Celtic ethnicity other than by shedding more light on the question of who the ancient Celts really were. Surely this makes more sense than clinging to ideas which have been shown to be based on some shaky eighteenth-century assumptions. A number of archaeologists, in what has been taken by some as deliberately provocation, have stated that they now think using the word 'Celtic' to denote anything to do with the British and Irish Iron Age is unhelpful since the word has become too loaded with meanings that have nothing to do with archaeology. However, this would have little impact on much modern usage of the word. The Scottish football team Celtic FC and the American basketball side the Boston Celtics are unlikely to be changing their names any time soon.

The Story in the DNA

The use of DNA analysis to investigate the genetic make-up of populations of people and, by extension, track changes in these populations and their movements, has developed to an extraordinary extent since the 1990s[15]. The methods involved are quite complicated but, in essence, involve tracking particular genetic markers (mutations in the DNA) which have been passed down through the generations of the population under investigation. This can be done separately through the female line, through which mitochondrial DNA exclusively flows, and the male line, by analysis of the DNA of the Y chromosome, only present in men. The frequency in the occurrence of mutations can be estimated, leading to the possibility of dating changes in the genetic composition of the overall population. This also allows geneticists to trace the movement of these mutations, going back over the course of thousands of years.

A detailed commentary on all aspects of this work is beyond the scope of this book but analyses independently carried out by both Brian Sykes and Stephen Oppenheimer have come to similar conclusions. The majority of the DNA in the populations of both Britain and Ireland has descended from the Mesolithic (Middle Stone Age) hunter gatherers who reoccupied the islands from what is now Spain and Portugal after the end of the last Ice Age, beginning about 12,000 years ago. Stephen Oppenheimer puts it in the following way:

> Much of the genetic input into north-west Europe derives from re-expansion from Iberian refugees after the Last Glacial Maximum (LGM), and before the start of the European Neolithic 7,500 years ago[16].

Oppenheimer goes on to estimate that approximately 60 – 70% of the genes in the populations of Britain and Ireland came from the Iberian peninsula during this period and, while there are many regional differences, these are outweighed by the similarities. He also identifies the Basque region of northern Spain as one of the main sources of these genes.

Subsequent gene flows into the islands have been relatively minor in comparison to the original influx, with no more than 5% of genetic material coming from any other particular place. This very obviously contradicts the Celtic invasion theory, as it does the once widely held belief that agriculture was brought to Britain and Ireland by people originating in the Near East and the equally widely held theory that the Anglo-Saxon occupation of England after the withdrawal of the Romans in the fifth century completely displaced the Celtic inhabitants of this area. All these events have left genetic traces, as have Viking incursions in the ninth and tenth centuries and the Norman invasion of 1066, but the lasting genetic impact has been no greater than immigration into Britain over the last 50 years.

Taken at face value this research suggests greater genetic similarities between all the peoples of Britain and Ireland than differences, whether or not these people regard themselves as being Celtic or Anglo-Saxon. While recognising this, Oppenheimer postulates a cultural divide between the Celtic lands and England which goes back much further than the arrival of the Anglo-Saxons in the fifth century AD. He suggests that what we now think of as the Celtic regions were made up of distinct communities and these were much more connected with each other than they were with what is now England. He also speculates on the possibility that the tribes in the south east of England spoke a Germanic language, related to the language of the Belgic tribes in what is now northern France and Belgium, rather than a dialect of the Celtic languages. This would put the first appearance of a proto-English language at a much earlier date than is currently thought to be the case and points towards a further instance of a separate cultural identity for the Celts. A certain amount of linguistic evidence backs up this theory but, at present, it is not widely accepted.

Archaeology, Genes and Myths

In his brilliant book *Facing the Ocean*, Barry Cunliffe provides extensive details of the archaeology of what he describes as the Atlantic façade of north-west Europe. He describes a continuity in the cultures of this region going back to something like 8,000 BC. But a complex picture also emerges in which the societies of this region are in a constant state of change, although, for the most part, the changes arise from within. This does not exclude influences from outside coming in, and Cunliffe also recognises the arrival of a relatively small number of immigrants, but the changes are not the result of the mass migrations of people.

Genetic investigations carried out in recent years come to very similar conclusions. It is true to say that these findings are not universally accepted in academic circles at present, and there have been other studies which have been interpreted in very different ways, but they certainly go some way towards supporting the archaeological theories. This research remains ongoing and will be the subject of a great deal of debate and, no doubt, some heated arguments before anything approaching a consensus is reached. In the meantime, the fact that similar conclusions have been reached in research conducted independently and through separate disciplines, and that the conclusions of one study (of the Celtic cultures of Britain and Ireland as a home-grown phenomenon) are not dependent on or even influenced by the results from the other study, means that the case is a convincing one.

Academic disciplines, like everything else, are subject to changing fashions and it could be argued this is what we are seeing at the moment. In the past any observable change in a culture was put down to the wholesale replacement of one group of people by another. These days the pendulum has swung to the opposite extreme and almost all cultural changes are described as the result of acculturation, the flow of ideas from one culture to another rather than the movement of people. Perhaps, at some point in the future, a middle position will be adopted which sees change occurring by both methods and by complex combinations of both.

The impact of these developing theories on a consideration of Celtic mythology is much the same as it is for the study of any other aspects of Celtic society in Britain and Ireland. If the arguments for a continuous culture are accepted, then rather than arriving with the Celtic peoples from central Europe 2,500 years ago, the Celtic tradition of storytelling, going back to pre-Christian times and (more than likely) much further back into prehistory, was an indigenous phenomenon. When dealing with the verbal products of an oral culture, it is impossible to know how far back into prehistory their origins go, but it would not be unreasonable to suggest that myths, in some form or another, arrived in Britain and Ireland with the Mesolithic hunter-gatherers as they came into the islands from refuges on the Iberian peninsula.

There are even allusions to Spain providing the origins of the Irish in some of the stories making up the eleventh-century Middle Irish collection known in English as *The Book of Invasions*, a translation of its Irish title *Lebor Gabála Erenn*. There is, of course, no way of checking the veracity of such sources and so drawing specific conclusions from them is not really possible. One of the stories concerns Breogán, the Milesian king of the Galician city of Brigantium (usually identified now as La Coruña), who built a great tower, so high that from the top he could see the distant green shore of Ireland. His sons went on an expedition to this new land but, once there, one of them was killed by the Tuatha Dé Danaan, the inhabitants of the country at that time. In revenge for this killing, one of Breogán's grandsons led a full invasion force to Ireland and defeated the Tuatha Dé Danaan in battle, thereby taking control of Ireland and becoming the ancestors of the modern Irish.

In light of the arguments set out above, there is a final question about Celtic mythology to consider. Is it still acceptable to give the stories that title? This book could, for example, be called *Vernacular Stories of the Atlantic Façade of North West Europe* or *Epic Narratives of the People Formerly Known as the Celts*, although, let's be honest, neither has much of a ring to it. Perhaps, in the absence of more suitable terminology, it would be best to stick with *Celtic Myths*.

Iron Age Society

It is only possible to speculate on the true antiquity of the surviving Celtic myths, to suggest they could be part of a tradition of storytelling going back thousands of years into prehistory, but what can be said for certain is that they predate the arrival of Christianity into Britain and Ireland in the fourth and fifth centuries AD. By the time the stories making up the mythologies were written down, they were already very old. From descriptions given in the stories of the types of weapons used in battle, and also from the use of chariots, it is possible to be fairly confident in stating that these stories relate to the Iron Age. This does not necessarily mean they were first composed in this period, but the versions recorded were in circulation at this time and, if they were older, they had been adapted for a contemporary audience. For present purposes, then, it is appropriate to consider society in general at this time, when, as an integral part of that society, storytellers were at work, telling their stories.

Iron was in use in Britain for thousands of years before the seventh century BC, when the Iron Age is conventionally said to have begun, but, up until the technology for producing iron had becoming relatively large scale, iron was rare and was only used to make ritual or ceremonial objects. By the seventh century BC, iron was being used regularly for more everyday objects, including tools and weapons, and this increasing use contributed to what we would now call a booming economy. Land clearance for farming, which had begun in the Neolithic, increased markedly, as did the population. It is difficult to estimate with any degree of accuracy but there were probably in the region of two to three million people living throughout the islands during this period.

Again conventionally, the Iron Age is said to have ended with the Roman invasion in AD 43, at which point, according to older history books at least, civilisation and history began in Britain. In those areas not occupied by the Romans, which correspond to the Celtic regions we know today and include the whole of Ireland, the Iron Age continued for about another 600 years, until the influence of Christianity became pervasive and Britain and Ireland entered what is sometimes called either the Early Medieval Period or the Dark Ages. As the mythology under consideration came from these areas, most of this discussion will concentrate on them, but it is worth bearing in mind that Roman Britain and the Celtic regions beyond its borders interacted with each other throughout the occupation. And, of course, the people living under Roman rule did not become Romanised overnight. Presumably they also had a tradition of story-telling but nothing at all of it survives. Those stories from England we do have, such as the epic poem *Beowulf*, are from a later time and, although (at least in the case of *Beowulf*) they appear to have more in common with Norse mythology, they are considered to be Anglo-Saxon in origin.

It is not strictly accurate to describe society in the Iron Age in Britain and Ireland as if it was a single entity, any more than it would be accurate to do so today. The islands were inhabited by various distinctive tribal groups, each occupying an area roughly equivalent to modern day counties but, despite this diversity, the tribes shared many cultural traits. Society was strictly hierarchical, with a nobility headed by a king or chief, a priesthood of what we now call druids, a warrior class, an artisan class and a large number of agricultural workers. In *The Gallic Wars*, Julius Caesar described these people as slaves, but he was most likely projecting a Roman view onto Britain. Slavery certainly appears to have existed but the slaves were most likely to have been prisoners taken by force during wars and raids rather than the common men and women who worked the land.

The majority of people in these agricultural societies lived on farmsteads, working the land in ways which would have been recognisable to farmers right up to the agricultural revolution of the eighteenth century. Where they have not been destroyed by later farming methods, Iron Age field systems show patchworks of small fields where cereal crops were grown and cattle, sheep and pigs were reared. Perhaps the main difference was that during the Iron Age almost all of the farmsteads were, to some degree, defended. Larger defensive structures were also constructed at this time, including hill forts such as Maiden Castle in Dorset and Danebury in Hampshire, where relatively large areas – about 40 acres in the case of Maiden Castle – were surrounded by networks of ditches and earth ramps, topped with wooden stockades.

In northern Scotland distinctive defensive structures called brochs, very solidly built stone towers, were a common feature, many of which survive to this day in various states of repair. On the Aran Islands, in Galway Bay, highly defended stone forts were built, including Dún Aonghasa on Innis Mór, dramatically perched on the edge of a cliff and with stone walls which are about 16ft (5m) thick. The obvious interpretation of the proliferation of such defensive structures is that the Iron Age was a volatile and unstable period, where wars between tribes were a common event and raids by one tribe on another an everyday hazard of life.

Another interpretation claims these fortifications were built as much for show as for protection, and suggests that the increasing power and wealth of the upper echelons of Iron Age society were expressed by the building of increasingly impressive structures, placed in dominant positions in the landscape. These were situated to be seen so that the local people were reminded who was in charge and any potential attackers were likely to think twice before approaching such obviously well-defended positions.

A further reason for the construction of these structures is demonstrated by the Scottish brochs. There are many more of them than was strictly necessary for defence alone and many of them have been built quite close together. What appears to have been happening was that the builders were competing with each other by ploughing increasingly large quantities of their resources into the building of unnecessarily elaborate brochs in order to show who was the wealthier. What started out being purely functional became a competition, suggesting an increasingly affluent society which could afford to waste resources in this way.

The truth of the matter may well lie in a combination of all the motivations outlined above. If the mythology is anything to go by, then fighting between tribes in one form or another was a common occurrence, although, since a fight is an inherently dramatic situation and more likely to be recorded than less dramatic ones, it could be that the stories in the mythology overstate the reality. The classical authors also describe the British tribes as prone to wars and fighting, both between themselves and with enemies from further afield, but these accounts are not those of impartial observers. Contact between the Romans and the British tribes was often when they were at war, so the accounts of Roman authors, written for a Roman readership, would obviously be heavily biased. The Romans tended to portray everyone but themselves as barbarians in need of the civilising hand of Rome so, while the tribes beaten in battle might suffer in the short term, it would do them good eventually because they would become part of the Roman Empire.

Roman authors often stress the wild nature of the warriors, describing them going into battle naked and working themselves up into a war rage before committing themselves to an all-out attack. This practice of getting into a violent frenzy before a fight is also attributed to Cúchulainn in the Táin, who becomes mad with fury before unleashing devastating attacks on his opponents. It also resembles the Scottish Highlanders charging at the massed ranks of the British Army of the Hanoverian Government at the end of the Jacobite Rebellion at the battle of Culloden in 1746.

Another practice of the Celtic tribes considered to be barbaric by the Romans was the decapitation of enemies after they were dead and the display of the heads by the victorious warriors. Archaeological evidence from continental Europe, and some limited finds in Ireland, gives credence to these descriptions, collections of skulls having been found in the excavations of Celtic houses. The display of the heads of victims may have been a sign of the prowess of a warrior in battle or possibly it could have had a religious significance, perhaps indicating taking possession of the souls of the enemy or even honouring the memory of dead opponents.

Battles between different tribes appear to have been quite formalised affairs, with ranks of warriors, often including women and children, facing each other, shouting abuse and boasting. The actual fighting was often limited to a small number of chosen champions from each side, who can be compared to the heroes found in the mythology. These confrontations have also been compared to a football match, with rival fans taunting each other and cheering on their side, although the intended outcomes of these encounters are rather different. Winning a match is not really on a par with cutting off an opponent's head. But the form of controlled warfare they practised enabled rival tribes to settle disputes without the deaths of large numbers of people and so avoided risking the long term survival of the tribes as a whole.

Large numbers of various different weapons and armour have survived in the archaeological record, having been placed in burials or apparently deliberately thrown into lakes and rivers as votive offerings. A number of complete chariots were recovered from burial sites in East Yorkshire, mostly dating to the fourth and fifth centuries BC. These correspond with similar chariot burials in northern Europe, but it is not known what level of contact they represent between Britain and Europe.

Many of the artefacts found have been highly decorated. The Battersea Shield, which was found in the Thames in London and is now in the British Museum, dates from the first century BC and was made from sheets of bronze decorated with enamel. The artistic work on the shield is in the La Tène style, characterised by decorative circles and swirls which have been hammered out from the inside in a metal-working technique called repoussé. It is generally thought that the weight of the shield, together with the fragility of its construction, would have made it almost useless if it had been employed in battle, so it probably had a ceremonial function, perhaps being specifically made to be thrown into the Thames as an offering to the gods.

Many of the swords found in lakes and rivers have been part of hoards, suggesting continued use of the same spot to make offerings or, in some cases, the disposal of a large number of weapons in one go, possibly those captured in battle. Some of these artefacts, like the Battersea Shield, are highly decorated and show no sign of use. The designs of these swords are similar to those found in many locations across Europe, suggesting an extensive trade network in these goods. They may also have been involved in the exchange of gifts between the nobility of different tribes to maintain friendly relations.

Another type of artefact which has been found in burials and in water is the torc, a type of heavy necklace made of precious metal, often gold, strands of which have been twisted together and bent to give the torc a characteristic crescent shape. These must surely have been accorded a high value and would have been worn by people of suitable status. When worn by men, it has been suggested, they could have been a sign of prowess in battle or perhaps a protective charm, but they were also worn by women, so it seems more likely they were a sign that the wearer belonged to the nobility.

The position of women in Iron Age Britain and Ireland appears to have been much more prominent than in the classical world. It has been suggested that this view has been over-promoted by modern feminists, attempting to emphasise the status of women, but there are plenty of accounts of women fighting in battle next to men and of them owning and inheriting goods and property. A well-known example of a powerful and prominent woman is

Boudica who, in the first century AD, became the queen of the Iceni, a tribe occupying what is now East Anglia, after her husband died and led an ultimately unsuccessful rebellion against the Romans.

The mythology also contains a number of examples of strong and powerful women. Here are just two examples from several in the Ulster Cycle. In the Táin, Mebh is the queen of Connacht and the leader of the attack on Ulster, the purpose of which is to steal a great bull. This is carried out because her husband, portrayed as her inferior, already owns a bull and she does not like to be outdone by him. In one of the early stories, a forerunner to the Táin itself, Deirdre, a woman at the court of Conchobar, the king of Ulster, is not prepared to submit to the commands of the king, who orders her to take the man who killed her lover for a husband. In doing this she challenges the strict honour code of the Irish heroes and finally dies rather than be dishonoured herself.

These two women are, of course, characters in stories, but it would seem reasonable to suggest that, for the stories to be effective, these strong independent women would have to be believable to the people listening. Whether such egalitarian principles applied to lower levels of society than the nobility is impossible to say, although there is no reason to think that women from the lower classes were not also capable of achieving a comparable status to their men.

Tara and Navan Fort

For some aspects of Celtic culture, the results of archaeological investigations and the details given in the mythology are, to some extent, in agreement. This is particularly the case with fighting and farming, two of the most prominent aspects of the culture. The stories in the mythology often concern fights of one sort or another and quite often it concerns one group stealing cattle from its neighbours who, unsurprisingly, take a dim view of this activity. One conclusion to draw from this is that great importance was attached to cattle in Celtic cultures, animals which are often held to be symbols of power and wealth in many agricultural societies.

Finding analogies between archaeology and mythology can be a dangerous occupation, not least because it is impossible to check the sources of the mythology or to date it with any accuracy. In general, details obtained from the mythology should only be used speculatively, as illustrations of possible scenarios that could arise from the interpretation of archaeological finds. However, there are some occasions when mythology and archaeology appear to support each other to such an extent that the similarities become impossible to dismiss. A number of such incidences are observable in Ireland and the discussion below uses two examples, the Hill of Tara and Navan Fort, to illustrate the point.

The Hill of Tara, in County Meath, about 20 miles north of Dublin, is one of the best known ancient sites in Ireland. It stands in the Boyne Valley, not far from other internationally important archaeological sites sometimes described as making up the ritual landscape of the Bend in the Boyne and including the passage tombs of Newgrange, Knowth and Dowth. A recent archaeological guide to Ireland has this to say about Tara:

An extraordinary convergence of history, literature, and archaeology reveals the Hill of Tara to be the centre-piece of a larger ritual and settlement landscape; defined and protected by religious and military monu-ments, taboos, and traditions, it became the *ferann rig* or royal estate of the kings of Tara during the early Middle Ages.[17]

Tara is named as the seat of numerous kings of Ireland, both mythological and historical, and features in many of the myths themselves, including the Ulster Cycle and *The Book of Invasions*. To take just one example from the Fenian Cycle, the youthful hero Fionn mac Cumhaill first proves himself by protecting Tara from Aillén mac Midgna, who comes to the hill at the same time every year, the Celtic festival of Samhain on 1st November, and on each occasion causes havoc in the same way. He lulls the men of Tara to sleep by playing music to them and then burns their houses to the ground. In return for being recognised as the head of his clan by the king of Tara, Fionn promises to take on Aillén. He makes himself immune to the sleep-inducing properties of the music and, after Aillén puts everyone else to sleep, fights and defeats him, cutting off his head and displaying it on the end of a spike. From that point onwards, Fionn becomes a hero and goes on to perform many more feats.

The site itself does not reveal anything of Fionn's heroic deeds, but does show its importance in Irish prehistory, going back to about 3,500 BC. There are about 25 monu-ments of various different forms in the complex as a whole, one of the best known of which is the Lia Fáil, or Stone of Destiny, a standing stone with obvious phallic symbolism, which, stories relate, cries out when touched by the true king of Ireland. The stone is last said to have cried out when it was touched by Brian Boru when he became king of Ireland in 1002, although the actual stone now standing on Tara was probably erected by Irish nationalists in the late eighteenth century.

Another important archaeological site with mythological connections is known in English as Navan Fort. It stands on the top of a hill near Armagh in Northern Ireland. In Irish it is called Emain Macha and it is the place named in the Ulster Cycle as the seat of the king, Conchobar, during the period when the events related in the Táin are said to have occurred.

The site initially appears to be that of a standard hill fort, protected by earth banks and ditches, but archaeological excavations have revealed it to be much more complex. The buildings on the top of the hill give the impression of being more ceremonial in purpose than defensive and the remains of an Iron Age roundhouse show that it was repeatedly burned down before being rebuilt. Archaeologists, including Francis Pryor, suggest that this is a royal residence and it has, together with other features of the site, a symbolic significance which relates to the transition from the realm of the living to that of the dead, the realm of the ancestors. This, they think, also relates to other circular monuments, built in Britain and Ireland over a period of many thousands of years. Pryor goes on to say:

> Certain places have roots that go back a long way, but the ideas, stories, myths and legends that make these places so special have origins that can ultimately be

traced through the Neolithic period and possibly even earlier. If archaeology teaches us anything, it is that thoughts and ideas can outlive the most permanent monuments.[18]

It is fanciful to suggest that such figures from mythology as Conchobar and Cúchulainn actually lived at Navan Fort. But, putting rationality aside for a minute, who is to say that one of the numerous burial sites around the hill don't contain the mortal remains of one of Ireland's greatest mythological heroes?

Religion

Attempting to reconstruct what people who lived in an oral culture were thinking some 2,000 years ago is an all-but-impossible task, so it is difficult to give specific details about the pre-Christian religion of Britain and Ireland. All we have left in words are the remnants of the mythology, mostly cleansed of any pagan religious associations in the early Christian period. Archaeology and the classical sources can increase our knowledge, but, in the end, both are interpretations made from a distance rather than direct links to the reality.

In *The Gallic War*, Julius Caesar described the Celts as a very religious people. He was referring to the people of Gaul rather than the Britons, so it does not necessarily follow that the people of Britain and Ireland were so inclined, but the evidence we actually have tends to suggest religion was a central part of their lives as well, informing and directing everything they did.

The Celtic religion, now often called paganism simply because it was not Christian, was a form of polytheism and its huge pantheon of gods and goddesses were associated with different aspects of the natural world – the sky, the sun, rivers, mountains and many others. Some of these deities were worshipped widely, across tribes and in what we would now think of as different countries, and some were local, specific to a tribe or to a particular location. The practice of this religion essentially appears to have involved making offerings to the chosen god or goddess in order to gain favour, which would then manifest itself in such forms as a successful harvest or victory in battle. If the mythology is anything to go by, then no undertaking, large or small, was begun before the favour of the gods and goddesses had been obtained, often leading to long delays until the required response was obtained.

The link between the mortal world and the realm of the gods was made by the priesthood, known now as druids, although the antiquity of this term is disputed and it seems unlikely they would have been called this at the time. Almost nothing is known for certain about them, with most current notions coming from the modern version of druids, seen at Stonehenge at the solstice and at other neo-pagan events. Although adherents of the various New Age religions do not see it this way, this has more to do with the imaginations of Celtic Revivalists, such as John Aubrey in the seventeenth century and William Stukeley in the eighteenth century, than it does with the actual Iron Age religion. Another well-known modern idea of the druid is represented by Getafix in the long-running *Asterix* cartoon series. He was always shown dressed in long white robes and had a matching long white beard, and was often seen cutting mistletoe with a golden sickle or brewing up another cauldron of magic potion. With the exception of the magic potion, Goscinny and Uderzo, the writer and illustrator of *Asterix*, based the details of the druid on descriptions given in the classical sources.

The druids were a secret order and passed the knowledge they possessed on to initiates entirely by oral means, so there is no way of knowing exactly what they did or how they went about it. They appear to have formed what is often called a brotherhood (although women could also become druids) and kept in touch with each other by holding regular meetings. There was a hierarchy, involving specific duties performed by different druids. Some probably specialised in certain fields while others had a more general role. As well as dealing with religious matters, they could also be philosophers, keepers of knowledge, seers, and arbiters of the law, and could fulfil a wide range of other functions. They may also have been involved in the telling of stories, although it is more likely this was the province of the bards.

The classical sources give accounts of the druids conducting human sacrifice. While they were certainly involved in making offerings to the gods and goddesses, it is not known if these included people. This could be another example of Roman propaganda, presenting their enemies as uncivilised barbarians, but, on the other hand, there are some indications human sacrifice could have occurred. One strand of evidence comes from interpretations of some of the numerous bog bodies found in Britain and Ireland as well as in other parts of northern Europe.

These are the bodies of people, mostly dating to the Iron Age, found in peat bogs, preserved by the particular conditions of acidity and the absence of air found in these environments. Many show the signs of having been violently killed, including the well-known examples of the Lindow Man, found in Cheshire in 1984, and Clonycavan Man, recovered from a bog in County Meath in 2003. Lindow Man, who died in the second century BC, was killed by three blows to the head. He then had his throat cut and was garrotted with a knotted rope. Somebody apparently wanted to make sure he was dead, although it has also been suggested that there was a ritualistic aspect to the killing. The idea of triplism, of things happening in threes, had sacred connotations.

Interpretations of these bog bodies differ widely, but the most usual ones assume that the victims were either convicted criminals or prisoners of war who were executed or killed as a sacrifice. Possibly their deaths were a combination of execution and sacrifice. Placing the bodies in bogs, where they would be preserved, was probably intentional, perhaps because these places were thought of as liminal, between earth and water, and thereby represented a sort of limbo state between the world of the living and the realm of the dead. If this were the case, then these people were, according to the Celtic religion, being prevented from entering the Otherworld, the realm of the ancestors and the gods and goddesses, when they died.

This Otherworld was, it is thought, underground and bodies of water, such as lakes and rivers, represented a transitional zone between it and the human zone. Throwing precious objects, such as ceremonial swords and jewellery, into lakes and rivers could have been a way of directly appealing to the deities who lived in the Otherworld. Sacred sites in general appear to have played an important part in the religion and, as well as making offerings by throwing things into specific bodies of water, druids conducted ceremonies in particular groves of trees, usually made up of oak, hazel and yew.

Festivals were also an important part of religious practice, many of which marked the important seasonal and agricultural events of the year. The four main festivals were called different names in different parts of the Celtic world and what follows is the Irish version, but these had equivalents in the other regions.

Imbolc was at the beginning of February, a time associated with ewes starting to produce milk, a sign they were about to lamb and that winter was finally coming to an end. The festival was dedicated to the goddess Brigid, becoming St Brigid's Day in the later Christian calendar. This was followed by Beltane, on 1 May, when livestock were taken out to their summer pastures. (This still remains a holiday in many countries, although often marking International Labour Day rather than anything to do with the Celtic calendar.) Lughnasa was celebrated on 1 August and was dedicated to the god Lugh. This was the beginning of the harvest season when people would make offerings to ensure a successful outcome. In the Christian calendar, thanks are given after a successful harvest has been brought. This illustrates one of the differences between polytheistic and monotheistic religions. In polytheism, offerings are made to deities before an event has occurred to ensure its success, while in monotheistic religions, in which a benevolent god is thought of as looking after the followers, offerings are made after the event as a sign of gratitude.

The last festival of the Celtic calendar was Samhain, on 1 November, marking the end of summer and the start of winter. This was the traditional time for slaughtering cattle, rather than feeding them over winter, and was marked by the lighting of bonfires. It can be seen as the forerunner of the English tradition of Bonfire Night, on 4 November, and it is also All Saints' Day in the Christian church, when the faithfully departed are commemorated. The evening before is now celebrated as Halloween, the name deriving from a corruption of All Hallow Even, the evening before All Hallows' Day, an old name for All Saints' Day.

Both the Romans and early Christians incorporated aspects of the Celtic religion into their own, but both also recognised the power of the druids and attempted to suppress their activities. The Roman author Strabo, for example, tells of an attack on the druids on Anglesey, apparently an important location for the druids, where they were defeated by the legions and their sacred groves were destroyed.

In various stories describing how St Patrick brought Christianity to Ireland in the fifth century, he is depicted debating with the druids and finally defeating them at the Hill of Tara, perhaps the most sacred place in the whole of the country. Whether the defeat of the druids was entirely down to St Patrick is open to question but, with the adoption of Christianity, the old Celtic religion began gradually to die out. The knowledge held in the minds of the druids was lost over time, until the only tangible connection with the old religion became the mythology, although the fact that the Catholic Church in Ireland recognises numerous Saints' Days and that certain locations are thought of as sacred could be a result of the incorporation of some of the old ways into Christian Ireland.

The Spoken and Written Word

Oral Tradition

One of the key aspects of Celtic myths is the relationships the surviving written stories have to the oral culture in which they were generated. At the point when they were written down, the stories became fixed, a part of the literary tradition rather than the spoken one. Prior to that, there must have been a long period when the stories survived and continued to be told through being passed down the generations by word of mouth.

A great deal of academic work has been done on the development of oral traditions of storytelling, going back to Milman Parry in the 1930s and later Albert Lord, who continued Parry's work on the oral components in Homer and extended it to consider how the oral poets of Yugoslavia (now Serbia), then working in a surviving tradition, went about the business of composing and performing their epic poetry.[19] It would be ridiculous to assume that the Homeric epics and Celtic myths were composed in exactly the same way, but, at the same time, both they and the Yugoslavian oral poetry were all the products of exclusively oral traditions, so it is not unreasonable to draw some comparisons. But, before going on to do that, it is necessary to consider what we mean when we talk of an oral culture and look at the differences between it and a written one.

Conceiving of how people lived before the invention of writing from the standpoint of modern Western culture, in which writing has become such an integral part that it is rarely remarked upon, is not easy. In terms of the overall history of humanity, writing is a relatively recent innovation. Recognisably modern humans (*Homo sapiens*) have been around for something like 200,000 years, while the earliest known writing system dates back to the Sumerian civilisation in Mesopotamia about 6,000 years ago. From its earliest use, it would be some thousands of years more before it became widespread and it would not be until the invention of the printing press with movable type in the fifteenth century (several centuries earlier in China) that books and literacy in general began to have the impact they have today. In his ground-breaking book *Orality and Literacy,* Walter Ong writes, 'More than any other single invention, writing has transformed human consciousness'[20]. It is an arguable point, but nevertheless gives an indication of the gulf between the way people think in oral cultures and the way they do so in written ones.

In a written culture complex ideas can be worked out on paper, one step at a time, and it is obviously possible to refer back to each stage by reading the notes. As this process continues a body of knowledge builds up, available to anybody who chooses to read it. This is, of course, not an option in an oral culture, so a central question arises. How do people in an oral culture work out difficult problems and then retain the knowledge they have gained?

One way problems are solved without the use of writing is through somebody having an inspired idea, the eureka moment, although such occasions cannot be predicted. Another way is to talk the problem over with somebody else, by dialogue in other words, and then to remember the solution by constantly repeating it or by developing a system of memory aids, or mnemonics, so that it can be remembered more easily. Where a large amount of information is concerned, such as in the extensive body of stories making up a mythology, learning it by rote and then retaining it all over a long period of time would be extremely difficult and, in an oral culture, if anything is forgotten, it is lost forever. A system of memory aids can overcome this problem and can also make passing on the information to the next generation more effective once the method of remembering has been taught.

One of the best ways of remembering a large amount of information is to associate what is to be remembered with specific locations, like stages on a journey or rooms in a house. Essentially what is happening here is that the information is being turned into a story, involving, say, going into your own house and moving from room to room. Each room, or particular objects in that room, bring back the specific bits of information associated with them. It becomes much easier to remember what might be otherwise unconnected pieces of information by placing them into the context of an unfolding story.

Recent scientific research suggests the human brain unconsciously generates stories all the time in an attempt to make sense of what might otherwise be a series of random or chaotic events.[21] Without our being aware of it, the

brain shifts through the enormous amount of sensory information coming in to it, discards what is considered unnec-
essary and strings the rest together in a form we can
understand. At present this is only a theory but, if this is the
case, then it is hardly surprising that we are predisposed to
remember information in the form of stories, because the
brain habitually perceives the world in this way.

In most oral traditions around the world, stories are
told in a verse form rather than as a prose narrative. This is
because it is easier to remember information when it is
placed within a regular repeating structure, where the
rhythm of the verse allows an oral poet to get into the flow
of the words. Other characteristics of verse, such as rhyme
and alliteration, can have similar functions, as well as acting
as memory aids in their own right. Almost the entire body
of Celtic mythology is, however, in prose, although this
may be more to do with the method by which it came to
be written down rather than because it was composed in
prose by oral storytellers in the first place.

Research on the Slavic tradition of oral poetry, which
existed into modern times, was initially aimed at shedding
light on how the Homeric epics were composed. The oral
poets studied made no attempt to memorise their entire
repertoire, which could run to many thousands of lines
and, if attempted, would have taken days to recite in full,
but learned the technique of composing verses as they
went along. They used numerous stock phrases to keep the
poem going and the rhythm regular, but also as memory
aids. Essentially they were improvising verse between
points in the story they knew they had to reach in order for
the narrative to work. Each performance of the same story

would, then, be different from the last, as most of the lines were composed as the poets went along, but ended up each time in the same place, unless the poet made changes to accommodate a particular set of circumstances, for instance to include topical material relevant to the audience. Both *The Iliad* and *The Odyssey* share these features of regularly repeated phrases, leading to the obvious conclusion that they were originally oral poems themselves.

The occurrence of repeated phrases is not so apparent in the Celtic myths simply because they were mostly first written down in prose. Some short passages of the Táin, however, are in verse. These are considered to be the parts written down at the oldest date, so they are those that, in all likelihood, most closely resemble the original oral version. While there are not enough verses to draw too many conclusions on the use of repetition, there are some instances of what were probably the use of stock phrases in the constant use of epithets after the names of the hero or, on occasion, to replace the name entirely. Cúchulainn is, amongst other names, referred to by a range of different names, all meaning the Hound of Ulster, in much the same way as Achilles is called by such epithets as the Breaker of Horses in *The Iliad*.

A further point of comparison between the longer examples of the Celtic stories and the Homeric epics, and long oral poems in general, is their episodic nature. Rather than following a linear plot, as a modern detective novel usually does, orally composed epics move from one incident to another. One reason for this is that the epics have developed over time and in repeated tellings, with some parts being added and, no doubt, other parts omitted.

Another point is that these stories, as well as relating epic events, can reach epic lengths, so, to keep the audience interested and involved over what could be a long stretch of time, each section of the story has its own climaxes. These episodes then build on each other to become parts of the overall story.

Similarities in the structure of literature from different places and times, such as those given above, provide an indication of the possibility that they were composed in the same way, but they should not be taken as any sort of absolute proof. Accounts of storytellers from modern times do not necessarily demonstrate how the stories making up an ancient mythology were composed, but they can also provide more circumstantial evidence. Seán de Búrca described a performance he witnessed by a traditional storyteller in Galway in the early 1970s as containing 'various expressions which occur repeatedly while adding virtually nothing to the tale itself'. He went on to say:

> From this duplication and redundancy, it is obvious that the brevity which exists in the tale has not been sought systematically. The impression given is one of composition during performance: of the transmitter fashioning his story (largely in his own words) from its basic elements as he goes along.[22]

The impression gained by de Búrca was, apparently, confirmed by the storyteller, so it is at least possible to say that this technique of composition has been used in Ireland at some stage.

The Storytellers

In this age of mass media and information technology, the art of storytelling is an entertainment form from the past and may be seen by some as folksy and nostalgic, no longer relevant to the world we live in. But, despite such opinions, storytelling is alive and well and, if anything, enjoying something of a resurgence. This is nowhere more apparent than in Ireland, where the storytellers continue to ply their ancient trade. One of the best known of these modern *seanachaithe,* as they are known in Irish, is Eddie Lenihan from County Clare who has collected stories over many years from the older generations of men and women from the west of Ireland and, as well as giving performances in many different countries, has written a number of books.

Like many folk traditions from around the world, storytelling has suffered from a perception that it is old-fashioned and stuck in the past, particularly by those who consider themselves too sophisticated for such homespun entertainment. To some people outside Ireland, who fail to see beyond stories of leprechauns and the little people, it has been taken as another stereotypical example of the superstitious Irish. Such attitudes have, of course, mostly changed in more recent times, both within Ireland and within the huge worldwide diaspora with its resurgent interest in Irish culture and 'Irishness'. Irish storytelling has followed a similar, if not quite so successful path, as Irish music, which has enjoyed something of a renaissance since the 1960s, led by bands like The Chieftains and Planxty.

As traditional as the *seanachaithe* are, it is impossible to say to what extent they are the inheritors of the tradition of storytelling going back to pre-Christian Ireland. At that time the storytellers, or *filid*, held a similar status to the druids and may actually have been a part of the same order, as they were the custodians of important oral knowledge relating to such subjects as ancestry, the law and codes of behaviour, held in the form of songs and narrative. The traditional role of the *filid* continued after Ireland became Christian, surviving the demise of the druids as the spiritual leaders of Ireland. They continued to work within the houses of the Irish nobility but, as the indigenous Irish nobility declined under pressure from the Church and, after their arrival in 1171, from Anglo-Norman barons, so too did the traditional storytellers.

By the seventeenth century the tradition of the *filid*, along with the Irish nobility that supported it, had almost entirely disappeared. Storytelling did not completely end, of course, but continued among the Irish-speaking community, particularly in the west of Ireland, where they were furthest from the influence of the English language. The terrible famines of the 1840s and early 1850s had a devastating impact on the Irish speaking communities, killing, it is thought, something like a million people and causing huge levels of emigration. By 1900, the population of Ireland had halved, from about 8 million to 4 million, a position from which it has never fully recovered. The Irish language, and along with it the storytelling tradition, suffered similarly, surviving only on the fringes of the country, but neither was ever entirely lost.

The situation in the other Celtic regions was broadly similar, with the languages declining in the face of English cultural domination. In Scotland, the defeat of the Jacobite

Rebellion and the Highland Clearances of the eighteenth century had a dramatic effect on the Scottish Gaelic speakers. Storytelling continued after this period, again particularly at the fringes and notably in some regions where there were large Gaelic-speaking immigrant communities, such as on Cape Breton Island in Nova Scotia, Canada.

In Wales, despite its proximity and the length of time it has been united to England (going back to the defeat of Llewellyn ap Gruffydd by Edward I in 1282), the language has survived to a greater extent than any of the other Celtic languages has done. A comparable bardic tradition to the *filid* of Ireland, known variously as the Poets of the Princes (*Beidd y Tywysogion*) and the Poets of the Nobility (*Cywyddwyr*), declined in much the same way. It is possible to trace the roots of the modern Eisteddfod, a festival of Welsh music and literature, back to this time, although the modern form is actually part of the Celtic Revival.

The last Cornish speaker is generally said to have been Dolly Pentreath, who died in 1777, although the language continued to some extent for many years after that, certainly up until the late nineteenth century when efforts were being made to revive it. The Manx language continued for longer, with the last native speaker dying in 1974, by which time the revival had been ongoing for a sufficient time for the language to have firmly re-established itself. Some of the younger Manx speakers could now reasonably be described as native speakers as it is the language they use on a day-to-day basis.

In Brittany, the Breton language was widely spoken up until the 1960s, despite considerable pressure from the French Government to replace it with French. Since then it has suffered a catastrophic decline, followed by a steady recovery, although the government continues to offer little support. Unfortunately, as has been the case in all the Celtic regions, while the language can be revived, once the folklore has been lost it is gone forever. There is no way of recovering an oral culture which relies on memory and an unbroken passage through the generations to survive. A huge body of recordings of folktales and reminiscences of older generations, who lived in a time when storytelling was still widely practised, have been made and, as mentioned at the beginning of this section, some storytellers are still working, but a great deal more has been lost.

The Written Story

Elements of an ancient mythology can certainly be traced in the folk tales remaining after the decline, and in some cases extinction, of the Celtic languages, but what would now be considered as the majority of the canon consists of stories written down between the seventh and twelfth centuries in Ireland.

Writing existed in Ireland before the arrival of Christianity in the form of the ogham script, found in short inscriptions on memorials or territorial markers, but not in any more substantial writing. Christianity is very much a literate religion, being based on the study of the scriptures and Bible reading. It arrived in Ireland from Britain in the fifth century, traditionally said to have been brought by St Patrick, although, in reality, a number of Christian missionaries were at work during that period. It spread throughout Ireland rapidly, replacing the former religion and the druids in a few generations, and literacy came with it, at least for those people attached to the monasteries.

Celtic Christianity developed along different lines to Christianity in continental Europe, where the faith had originally spread through the Roman Empire. Rather than an administrative structure based around the cathedral and diocese, overseen by a bishop, in Ireland a mostly monastic system developed. One of the primary reasons for this was that Ireland remained almost entirely rural at this time, without the structure of cities and towns on which the Roman system relied. Cathedrals were, in the main, built in cities and paid for by the ruling elite from the proceeds of trade, while the monasteries of Ireland and their abbots were associated with the patronage of the Irish nobility, an institution which was essentially rural in nature.

The monasteries were, as well as religious institutions, centres of learning, where Greek and Latin were being read and written, and Irish monks so developed the art of copying the scriptures that they were unrivalled in the rest of Europe. The high point of this work came in about the ninth century, culminating in *The Book of Kells*, a superbly illustrated and ornate manuscript of the four gospels now in Trinity College Library in Dublin. The work of these scribes was not exclusively limited to religious matters, as the vast array of surviving manuscripts shows. The majority of the stories we have come from this source.

It is impossible to say for certain now to what extent the monastic scribes co-operated with the *filid* on the production of these texts. Both were associated with the patronage of noble houses and the *filid* may well have had some direct involvement in the monasteries themselves, even to

the point of writing manuscripts, but the evidence is simply not there to say for sure. Some of the texts give the
impression that they were prepared for the purpose of
being read aloud, or, at least, that they were rather like
prompt books for actors who have forgotten a line, but
most would appear to have been prepared with a more
scholarly purpose in mind. Gerald Murphy, one of a number of eminent academics specialising in early Irish literature in the 1950s and 1960s, thought 'the manuscripts
were mainly monastic and scribes were interested in the
historic rather than the aesthetic value of the matter they
recorded', suggesting their primary concern was not how
the stories would be received if read to an audience.
Murphy also says:

> We can be fairly certain that the tales, as really told to
> assembled kings and nobles at an ancient oenach [a gath-
> ering where stories and songs were performed], were
> very different from the poorly-narrated manuscript ver-
> sions noted down by monastic scribes as a contribution
> to learning rather than to literature.[23]

Here Murphy is referring to some of the earlier manuscripts, which are confused and difficult to untangle, but
the point could equally as well apply to much of the surviving material. The scribes were not necessarily concerned with faithfully copying verbatim records of what
the *filid* were relating in the stories. They were simply putting down in writing the factual information contained in
the stories that were relayed to them.

Functional aims rather than artistic ones may also

explain why the majority of the tales were written in prose, in contrast to oral stories from most other parts of the world which were in verse. It is, of course, entirely possible that the *filid* composed in prose in the first place, which is what most academics in the field assume, but, from what evidence we have, performances of the stories were normally accompanied by music, played on, for instance, the harp, so it would make sense for a certain amount of rhythm to have been present in the words. If they were present at all, most of these verse forms were either not recorded in the first place or were gradually lost as successive copies of the manuscripts were made. Alternatively, the scribes may simply have been used to copying verses from Biblical texts which were set out in prose form and continued in the same way with the stories. A person writing down a record of an oral performance would not necessarily set it down in verse form, particularly if they were not familiar with that form in the first place.

At some stage in the process, most of the pre-Christian religious significance of the stories was omitted and, on some occasions, some overtly Christian themes inserted. This could have occurred at any stage, from the composing process of the *filid* to the recording process of the scribes, as both were working within a Christian environment. Yet perhaps the most surprising fact is that the scribes actually wrote down any of these stories at all. This suggests an integration between the clerical and secular worlds not in evidence anywhere else in the Christian sphere which was, perhaps, a result of the remoteness of Ireland from mainstream Christianity.

Monastic scribes certainly existed in other Celtic regions, such as at the monastery founded on the Scottish island of Iona by St Columba in 563, but, if any secular stories were recorded in these places, none have survived. The only other source of written stories obviously based on much older oral traditions of mythology comes from Wales and makes up what is now known as the Mabinogion. Little is known about the origin of these stories, which now only exist in copies made some centuries after they are thought to have been first written down. These must surely only represent a fraction of the whole, but this is more than for the rest of the Celtic world. It is inconceivable that Scotland, the Isle of Man, Cornwall and Brittany did not have a rich tradition of storytelling. What they did not have was a set of circumstances such as existed in Ireland, which resulted in the stories being recorded before the tradition declined.

The Celtic Revival

From the twelfth century, beginning with the Anglo-Norman invasion, indigenous Irish culture entered a long period of instability and decline. Increased contact with Europe in this period also led to the greater integration of Celtic Christianity with the Roman Church and the monasteries came more and more under the direction of European monastic orders, like the Dominicans and the Cistercians. The conditions which had led to the flourishing of learning in the Irish monasteries were no longer in place and their position as some of the foremost centres of European scholarship diminished.

By the beginning of the fifteenth century the Anglo-Normans, or Old English as they are sometimes called, had integrated into Irish society, now firmly Roman Catholic. The English kings of the period were nominally in control of the country but large parts of it, particularly in the rural areas, were in reality ruled by dynasties of Anglo-Norman and indigenous Irish families. The Tudor king Henry VIII began the re-conquest of Ireland in the 1530s and, in an attempt to secure the continuing support of the Irish nobility, strove to integrate them into the English aristocracy by offering them English titles. Any who resisted, particularly after the Reformation, when the Protestant Anglican Church was created and the Dissolution of the Monasteries took place, were persecuted.

Historians often point to the event known as the Flight of the Earls as a turning point in Irish history. In 1607, two of the most powerful of the remaining Catholic Irish nobles from the north of the country left for exile in France, hoping to return when conditions were right for them to resume power. Neither ever did come back. This opened the way for the colonisation of the north by English and Scottish Protestants in what is known as the Plantation of Ulster, the ramifications of which are still being felt to this day.

Those members of the Irish aristocracy who remained continued to exert some influence in other parts of the country and some of them mounted a rebellion in 1641, creating the Catholic Confederation. This led to a period of war within Ireland which lasted until the English under Oliver Cromwell defeated the Confederation in 1653. The brutality of the methods employed by Cromwell during the war and its aftermath, which, some historians argue, amounted to genocide, have made Cromwell a continuing figure of hatred in Ireland.

All of the lands remaining in the possession of the Irish Catholic aristocracy were seized after Cromwell's victory, whether they had been involved in the rebellion or not. The institution of the *filid*, which relied on the patronage of the nobility, effectively ceased to exist at this time, putting an end to an oral tradition stretching back for at least 2,000 years. The failure of the 1689 Jacobite rising in Ireland, aimed at restoring the Catholic James II to the English throne and including defeat at the Battle of the Boyne in 1690, can be seen as a final nail in the coffin of the Catholic Irish upper classes.

During the eighteenth century the Celtic cultures of Britain and Ireland were considered to be in terminal decline and it was thought that it would only be a matter of time before they became fully absorbed into the dominant English culture. The beginnings of a revival can be seen in a number of different cultural movements. One of them was Romanticism, in which the remaining Celts were imagined as the last embers of a once great empire stretching across Europe. Irish nationalists, including Daniel O'Connell (1775-1842), didn't quite see history in the same light. They used these Romantic evocations of a glorious past as a way of gaining support for a nationalist agenda in Ireland, which included Catholic emancipation and the dissolution of the union between England and Ireland. Meetings were held at the Hill of Tara, where Kings of Ireland had been crowned, and the heroes of Irish stories set up as models for the future of Ireland.

One of the events which would bring Celtic mythology

to the attention of a much wider public was the publication of the Ossian poems by the Scottish poet James Macpherson, beginning in 1760. Macpherson claimed these were translations from the Scottish Gaelic of manuscripts he had obtained while travelling in the west of Scotland. The poems included an epic written, according to Macpherson, by an ancient Scottish bard called Ossian about the deeds of Fingal. The authenticity of these poems was immediately questioned, including by no less a figure than Dr Johnson, but this did not stop them becoming immensely popular across Europe. Admirers included Sir Walter Scott and JW von Goethe and the poems influenced many contemporary works of art and formed the basis of a number of operas.

It has since been shown that these poems were created by Macpherson from a number of Scottish folktales, mainly based on the Irish stories of Fionn mac Cumhaill and his son Oisin, strung together with verses of his own invention. But, however fake the poems were, they created a huge interest in Celtic mythology, leading to a climate in which the genuine myths, languishing unread for hundreds of years, would be rediscovered.

In the meantime academics had recognised the similarities between the different Celtic languages and were working on theories connecting the Celtic world of Britain and Ireland with the cultures of central Europe. Later in the nineteenth century Irish writers, such as WB Yeats, Lady Gregory and JM Synge, united these disparate strands of scholarship, Romanticism and Irish nationalism, and came up with an artistic movement called the Irish Literary Revival. The work of these writers and artists was greatly influenced by Irish myth and folklore. The following quote comes from *The Wanderings of Oisin,* an early poem by Yeats:

> Caoilte, and Conan, and Finn were there,
> When we followed a deer with our baying hounds.
> With Bran, Sceolan, and Lomair,
> And passing the Firbolgs' burial-mounds,
> Came to the cairn-heaped grassy hill
> Where passionate Maeve is stony-still;
> And found on the dove-grey edge of the sea
> A pearl-pale, high-born lady, who rode
> On a horse with bridle of findrinny;
> And like a sunset were her lips,
> A stormy sunset on doomed ships;
> A citron colour gloomed in her hair.[24]

The influence of mythology, particularly the Fenian Cycle, is very clear in this poem. Yeats would later reject most of his early poetry, written in this rather overblown style, but he specifically did not disown *The Wanderings of Oisin*. His more mature poetry moved away from such romantic musings and he would become one of the most significant poets of the twentieth century.

The Irish Cycles

Overview

In all there are about 150 written stories which together make up the corpus of Irish mythology. All of these are contained in ten manuscripts, written from the twelfth century to the fourteenth century. Linguistic evidence suggests some of the stories were copied into the extant manuscripts from earlier manuscripts dating back to the seventh century, none of which now survive. One of the reasons for this is the turbulent history of Ireland in the ninth and tenth centuries, when the country in general and the monasteries in particular were the objects of frequent Viking raids. The Vikings were, of course, looking for anything valuable and would not have been particularly interested in monastic manuscripts unless they were illuminated, but, in the chaos of these times, a large number of manuscripts were lost.

The most important manuscripts we still have are the monastic codices, large leather-bound volumes mostly containing sheets of vellum, a type of parchment made from calf or sheep skin. The later codices are made up of sheets of paper. The manuscripts they contain are by no means all mythological stories. They are a miscellany, apparently in no particular order, of whatever the scribes who wrote in them considered of interest at the time.

The earliest surviving of these codices is known as *The Book of the Dun Cow* (*Lebor na hUidre*), originally created in the monastery of Clonmacnoise in County Offaly, not far from Athlone in the middle of Ireland, and is now held in the Royal Irish Academy in Dublin. The codex gets its name from a story saying that its vellum was made from a cow, presumably dun in colour, owned by St Ciaran of Clonmacnoise, who founded the monastery in 545. The codex itself can be dated with some degree of authority to the beginning of the twelfth century and it would appear unlikely that leaves of vellum would not have been used until more than 500 years after they were made.

In the majority of cases, the scribes of these early man-uscripts remain anonymous but, in the case of *The Book of the Dun Cow,* it is possible to put a name to the man who first wrote in it and was responsible for about 60% of the content. He wrote his name in the margin of one of the leaves in the course of a pen test. These were processes known by the Latin name *probationes pennae,* in which a scribe who had cut a new pen, from a goose or a reed, tested it to check it was writing properly before using it for the actual manuscript work. This particular scribe was called Máel Muire mac Céileachair who, it is known from a later chronicle, came from a long line of clerics at Clonmacnoise, going back almost to the date of the monastery's foundation. We also know he was killed in a Viking raid on the monastery in 1106, so obviously most of the manuscripts in the codex were written before this date.

Before the codex came into the possession of the Royal

Irish Academy in 1844 it appears to have had a rough life, having been damaged on a number of occasions. It now contains 67 leaves of vellum, but clearly was much larger at some point in its history. Some of the stories it contains are incomplete and there must have been others which have been lost entirely. As it is, it contains the earliest known version of the Táin, along with numerous other stories, such as 'The Wooing of Étain' (*Tochmarc Étaine*) and 'The Voyage of Bran' (*Imramm Brain*).

The other major early source of stories is known as *The Book of Leinster* (*Lebor Laignech*) and is now held in the library of Trinity College Dublin. Although it is not possible to be as precise about its history as that of *The Book of the Dun Cow*, it is generally held to date from about 1160 and to have come from a monastery in County Wexford. It is in better condition than the codex from Clonmacnoise, but is still thought to be missing some leaves. It contains, amongst many other things, the most complete known version of the Táin, as well as *The Book of Invasions* and a large collection of bardic verse known as 'The Metrical Dindshenchas'. Bardic verse was composed by the *filid* as part of their duties to the household where they worked and usually consisted of praise poems to the head of the house, together with complicated genealogies and items of news. A large body of these poems has survived, although much of it is obscure and would require serious scholarship to unravel what is being related.

The stories contained in these two manuscripts, and in later ones such as *The Yellow Book of Lecan* and *The Great Book of Lecan*, offer different versions of the same myths. These different versions are known as recensions. The version of the Táin in *The Book of the Dun Cow* is, for example, known as Recension 1 because it is the earliest. Most modern English translations make use of a number of the recensions in an attempt to give as full a rendering of the narrative of the story as possible from all the sources.

The myths themselves are usually divided into groups of stories which have similar themes and these groupings are known as the cycles. This has nothing to do with the way the stories were ordered in the codices, which mostly appears to be random, but is the result of the work of German academics in the nineteenth century, who deciphered the Old Irish grammar of the stories, allowing them to be translated, and recognised those stories with common themes. We now recognise four cycles; the Ulster Cycle, the Fenian Cycle, the Mythological Cycle and the Cycles of Kings, sometimes known as the Historical Cycle. To take one example, the Ulster Cycle consists of about 80 stories in all which concern the heroic deeds of the Ulaid, the people of the north east of Ireland who gave their name to the province. Most, but by no means all, concern the life of Cúchulainn and the seemingly endless number of fights he got into.

As well as the four cycles, there are a number of stories which do not readily fit with the themes and these are usually considered separately. These are sometimes characterised as the *Echtrae*, stories concerning a hero's adventures in the Otherworld, and the *Immrama*, the voyage stories.

The Ulster Cycle

The 80 stories of the Ulster Cycle vary widely in length, from those of a page or two of prose to the longest, the Táin, which is what we might now think of as book length. Because of its length and its central position in the canon of Irish literature, the Táin will be examined separately in a later section. This section considers the Ulster Cycle in general and a number of the stories in particular.

The stories revolve around the exploits of the nobility and warrior classes of the Ulaid, the people of Ulster, and their king Conchobar mac Nessa, who rules from Emain Macha, now known in English as the archaeological site of Navan Fort. As well as the heroic deeds of Cúchulainn, the stories feature a number of other recurring characters. Fergus mac Róich is another heroic warrior who, in line with Ulaid tradition, has taken Cúchulainn into his household as a foster son, as he has done Conall Cernach and Ferdiad. The stories of all these, along with a host of others, intertwine with recurrent themes and actions which reveal other aspects of the characters' lives. Despite these common themes, the stories, or at least the ones we have, don't form a continuous narrative. They are more like a string of related, but separate, episodes.

It has been suggested that the stories originally recounted actual events, occurring at a specific time in history, which, if strict definitions were being followed, would make them legends rather than myths. In a few of the stories, such as 'The Death of Conchobar', the time scale of events is actually given in the text, relating them to the death of Christ, but this would appear to have been an addition of the monastic scribes who wrote the stories down. These scribes are sometimes referred to in the academic literature as the 'redactors' because of their presumed role in shaping the stories for the Christian era within which they worked.

The language of the stories can be linguistically related to the seventh century, but many are apparently some centuries older than this as the descriptions given in the texts often relate to the Iron Age. The warriors fight in single combat, as champions of their respective people. They engage each other with swords and spears, sometimes from the backs of chariots drawn by two horses and driven by a charioteer. The archaeological record has yet to show any evidence of chariots in Ireland in this period, although this may say more about the state of our knowledge than the actual situation and, as Barry Cunliffe puts it, 'absence of evidence is not evidence of absence'.[25] Despite such qualifications, there can be little doubt that the stories are, in essence, pre-Christian. Kings are advised by druids, seers tell of the events of a story, usually involving the inevitable downfall of one of the protagonists, and poets and storytellers hold powerful positions in the courts of the kings, equivalent to that of the druids. Kenneth Jackson famously described the stories as being 'windows on the Iron Age'[26] and there is an element of truth in this although, again, the work of the redactors also has to be considered.

One of the best known of the stories, other than the Táin, is 'The Exile of the Sons of Uisliu', not least because it concerns the tragic heroine Deirdre, one of the most powerful of all female characters in Irish literature. Jeffrey Gantz, in the introduction to his translation of the story, describes it as 'one of the finest stories ever written in Ireland' and goes on to say that it:

> ... evinces much of what Irish literature is: romantic, idealistic, stylized and yet vividly, even appallingly concrete. Most of all, it exemplifies the tension between reality and fantasy that characterizes all Celtic art.[27]

The story begins with Conchobar and the Ulaid drinking in the house of the king's storyteller whose wife is pregnant. When she stands up to go to bed, the unborn child screams out, so loudly all the men can hear it over the noise of their drunken revelry. Cathbad, a druid, feels the woman's stomach and makes a prediction, saying, in one of the sections of verse in the story:

> In the cradle of your womb there cried out
> a woman with twisted yellow hair
> and beautiful grey green eyes.
> Foxglove her purple pink cheeks,
> the colour of snow her flawless cheeks,
> brilliant her Parthian-red lips.
> A woman over whom there will be great strife
> among the chariot-warriors of Ulaid.[28]

The storyteller's wife gives birth to a girl, who is called Deirdre, and Conchobar takes her to his house to raise her to become his companion. One winter day, while she is in Conchobar's house, she sees her foster father skinning a calf and watches while a raven drinks the blood spilled in the snow and says 'I could have a man with those three colours: with hair like a raven, cheeks like blood and body like snow.'

Naoise, one of the three sons of Uisliu, is such a man and, when the two meet, after initially mistaking her for a heifer, he begins to sing to her. The rest of the Ulaid, knowing the prophecy, are enraged and a great fight breaks out. Naoise and Deirdre flee Emain Macha, along with his two brothers and their large retinues. They find sanctuary with a king in Scotland, but, when the king hears of the great beauty of Deirdre, be begins to plot the death of Naoise. Conchobar hears of this and sends word to Naoise and Deirdre to come back to Emain Macha. They agree to go back when their safety has been guaranteed by Fergus mac Róich, Durthact and Conchobar's son Cormac, who all go to Scotland to escort them home.

As they are on the way Conchobar instructs people to offer Fergus constant hospitality and, together with Durthact and Cormac, Fergus is duty bound to accept. Naoise and Deirdre thus get back to Emain Macha without their guarantors and, immediately, Naoise is killed by a spear thrown by Éogan, the son of Durthact. The Ulaid kill the other two sons of Uisliu and Deirdre is forced to stand by Conchobar and become his consort. Fergus gets back after this has all happened and is outraged at this terrible slight to his honour. A terrible fight breaks out, in which one of Conchobar's sons is killed, and afterwards Fergus goes into exile in Connacht with 3,000 of his men, where he will be when the events of the Táin are played out.

Deirdre lives with Conchobar for a year but, in the whole time she is with him, she never smiles or laughs and is often found holding her head in her hands in her grief for the death of Naoise. Conchobar asks her whom she hates most and she says she hates both him and Éogan in equal measure. Conchobar replies that she must now spend a year with Éogan. The following day he takes her to meet Éogan in his chariot but, on the way, she leans out over the side and commits suicide by smashing her head against a rock.

This story in not at all typical of the stories in the Ulster Cycle. Cúchulainn does not feature at all and throughout the story Conchobar, who is normally depicted as a benevolent leader, is shown up as a grasping old man, jealous of the youth and good looks of Naoise which have attracted the woman he covets. One way of looking at it is to think of it as an example of a well known plot in mythology – that in which an old king, fighting against his declining powers, rages against the younger king who will soon replace him and clashes with him over the attentions of a woman, in this case Deirdre, who is a goddess in human form.

The story of Deirdre may not be typical, but the same could not be said for 'Briccriu's Feast'. In what is one of the longer stories, Briccriu, who is something of a trouble-maker and not unlike the classic trickster characters from many mythologies around the world, organises a great feast and goads three of Ulster's great champions, Lóegaire Búadach, Conall Cernach and Cúchulainn, into an unseemly competition to decide who will get the champion's cut, the choicest portions of meat and the seat at Conchobar's right hand. At first Briccriu's plan is thwarted by Conchobar's poet, who is a wise man and suggests dividing the champion's cut equally between the three warriors so that there will be no need for an argument.

Briccriu switches tack by going to each of the warrior's wives in turn before they have arrived at the feast and telling them that the first to enter his house will show she has a higher standing than the other two. The three women meet on the way to the feast and each one, not realising the others are at the same game, tries to get to Briccriu's house first, gradually walking faster and faster until they are all running as fast as they can. Lóegaire and Conal break down the door so their two wives can get in together and Cúchulainn breaks through the wall, half knocking the house down in the process, in an attempt to get his wife in first. Briccriu, understandably, is not happy about all the damage to his house, but the poet, acting as peacemaker again, gets Cúchulainn to fix it. This he does by flying into a rage, as he does before going into battle, picking the whole house up and putting it back down where it is supposed to be.

Everything calms down again, but the problem of who should get the champion's cut has not been resolved. At this point, you would think, sense might prevail, but it is a question of honour, a subject the three warriors take very seriously. They decide, rather surprisingly, to ask their arch-enemy, Queen Medb of Connacht, to help them find a solution and all the interested parties head off to see her. Ailill, Medb's consort, realises he has trouble on his hands when he is told about the problem. If he chooses one of the warriors, he will make the other two into his deadly enemies but, luckily for him, when the warriors are eating in his hall, three demonic cats are loosed into the hall with them. Lóegaire and Conall both escape the cats by climbing into the rafters, but Cúchulainn remains calm and carries on eating. Ailill thinks he has solved his problem and declares Cúchulainn the winner. The other two warriors, however, refuse to accept this and all three go back to Emain Macha with the problem still hanging over them.

More indecisive challenges follow so the three go to see the great warrior of Munster, Cú Roi, who is reputed to have magical powers. He sets them another challenge, to see who can prevent him getting into his own house. Cúchulainn is the winner once again but the other two will still not accept the outcome and they return to Emain Macha once more.

In the end, in a part of the story of a later date than the rest, a winner is found in a similar resolution to that of the fourteenth century English poem *Sir Gawain and the Green Knight*. A giant comes to Emain Macha and challenges all three warriors to a beheading contest. Each one gets a turn to behead the giant with an axe, but, if he fails, the giant then gets to behead him. Lóegaire and Conall each strike the head off the giant but, on both occasions, the body of the giant gets up and carries away his head. The following day he returns, his head fully restored. When the giant demands his turn with the axe, neither Lóegaire nor Conal can be found but, when the same thing happens to Cúchulainn, he offers his neck to the axe. The giant takes the axe but uses the blunt end and, instead of cutting Cúchulainn's head off, just touches his exposed neck. Cúchulainn is declared the bravest of the three and the giant reveals himself to have been Cú Roi all the time. Finally, the hero takes the champion's portion.

Some commentators consider that the ending has been adapted to fit the story and that it is not its natural conclusion. The beheading theme is a familiar one from a number of other stories as well as from *Sir Gawain*, so may have been known to the redactors of 'Briccriu's Feast', who stitched it on to an otherwise unfinished narrative. Whatever the truth of the matter, the final scene does provide the story with a sense of completeness lacking in many of the other myths.

Another feature of this story is its use of humour, poking fun at the ridiculous lengths the warriors are prepared to go to prove themselves and protect their honour. They might be heroes, but that doesn't mean they are immune from being the butt of a few jokes. The use of three brothers – as Lóegaire Búadach, Conall Cernach and Cúchulainn effectively are – is a common feature of Celtic mythology, where the number three is important. A story in which three brothers compete with each other at tasks which have been set for them and in which the youngest one, in this case Cúchulainn, eventually comes out on top is also a universal one in mythology and storytelling in general.

'Briccriu's Feast' also features one of the first accounts of Cúchulainn going into a frenzy, or 'warp spasm' as Thomas Kinsella translates the Old Irish word *ríastrad* in his English version of the Táin. The war rage of the Celts was commented on by Julius Caesar in *The Gallic Wars*, where he describes warriors issuing challenges and boasts while working themselves up into a fury before going into battle in a characteristic all-out charge. When Cúchulainn does it, he becomes endowed with superhuman powers. In 'Briccriu's Feast', he is capable of lifting a whole house on his own and, in other stories, of going on a killing frenzy, slaughtering untold numbers of his enemies.

The Hound of Culann

Many of the stories in the Ulster Cycle relate episodes from Cúchulainn's life, some of these in different and conflicting versions, but almost all focusing on his abilities as the ultimate warrior of the Ulaid, not unlike Achilles in *The Iliad*. The story of his birth obviously does not tell of his heroic deeds, but it is full of symbolism, not all of it well understood now, about what is to come. In one version of the story, the Ulaid, including Conchobar and his sister Deichtine (sometimes said to be his daughter) are out hunting a flock of birds which have been eating their crops. Birds, in Celtic mythology, are intermediaries between this world and the Otherworld because they can cross between the earth and the sky, and their sudden appearance and direction of flight were used by druids as portents of the future. What the birds in the story are signifying is not clear today, although it probably would have been to a pre-Christian audience.

The hunters followed the birds all day, ending up at Brugh na Bóinne, the Neolithic passage tombs at Newgrange, by nightfall, where they take shelter with a man and his very pregnant wife. During the night she gives birth to a boy, helped by Deichtine, who takes the child back to Emain Macha the next day as her foster son. The child sickens and dies and, when Deichtine takes a drink of water, she is so distracted with grief she doesn't notice as some sort of small creature slips into her mouth with the water, making her pregnant in the process (the sexual imagery here is obvious). In the night Lugh, a Celtic god associated with prowess in all things, appears to Deichtine in her dreams and tells her that he is the father of the child. Conchobar, perhaps to avoid the impression that the child is his, sends Deichtine to Sualtam who takes on the role of father when the boy later to become Cúchulainn is born.

As a youth Cúchulainn is known as Sétanta (now the name of an Irish TV sports channel, given that name because, when he is young, Cúchulainn often plays hurling). He spends periods of time as a foster son in the houses of a number of influential figures, including Conchobar and Fergus mac Róich, relationships that will stand him in good stead in later life. As with many great heroes, Sétanta must earn his warrior name and does so in what can be seen as a rite of passage. In one of the versions, which the scholar of Irish literature and folklore Dáithí Ó hÓgáin[29] considers to be from a secondary source (i.e. a story of later invention), Conchobar and the Ulaid visit the smith Culann, in whose house Sétanta was fostered at the time. The smith has a ferocious dog, trained to protect his property, and after the Ulaid have gone into his house, he lets the dog out to protect them against intruders, not realising Sétanta has not come in with them. Sétanta arrives back at the forge and is attacked by the great dog, which he kills by smashing its head against the stone door post of Culann's house. Everyone is relieved to find Sétanta has not been hurt, but Culann is deeply upset about the death of his dog. Sétanta, noticing the smith's distress, offers to guard the forge himself while he raises another dog to replace the one he has killed.

According to Ó hÓgáin, Cúchulainn's boyhood deeds, some of which are related by other characters in the Táin when they are talking about him, can be read as a kind of manual for training would-be warriors. Cúchulainn sets an example of the perfect warrior in his exploits and the way he behaves, a role model for boys wanting to become warriors themselves. But there is a price to be paid for his prowess, as, again, there was for Achilles. As part of a prophecy, the druid Cathbad tells him his name will live forever in Ireland if he accepts his fate to become a great warrior but, in doing so, he is condemning himself to a short life and early death. Cúchulainn accepts the price of his fame and goes on to fulfil the prophecy. Some two thousand years later the prophecy appears to be holding good.

In 'The Wooing of Emer', Cúchulainn's good looks and prowess in all things is causing trouble for other men of the Ulaid. They are worried about their wives and daughters, who are all infatuated with Cúchulainn. They decide it is time he got married, so all the women will forget about him, and they set out to look for a suitable bride. Cúchulainn, in the meantime, meets Emer and begins to flirt with her, saying he would like 'to rest his weapon in the sweet country of her breasts'. She responds by telling him that no man will travel in that country until they have completed the tasks she sets for them. Cúchulainn must kill a hundred men, one at each ford in the river Ailbine; perform the salmon-leaping feat, in which he must strike down three groups of nine men and yet leave the man in the middle of each group standing; and go sleepless through three seasons of the year, from November to the following August.

Cúchulainn accepts the challenge and he goes to Scotland to train for the tasks and to escape Emer's father and the rest of her family, who haven't taken much of a shine to him as a prospective husband. The women of Scotland react to him in the same way as the women of Ulster did and he has a number of amorous encounters. In one of these he fathers a son, who is born before he returns to Ulster and named Connla. Cúchulainn gives the boy a gold ring so he will know his son the next time they meet. (In another story, Cúchulainn later kills Connla in a fight, only seeing the ring after his son is dead.)

On his return from Scotland he takes on Emer's family and completes all the tasks she has set him. Although Cúchulainn is responsible for the death of her father, the two get married and, from then on, Emer is portrayed as always by his side. But this does not mean everything always goes smoothly for the couple. In 'The Sickbed of Cúchulainn' (a title The Pogues used for one of their songs) Cúchulainn is tempted by Fann, an Otherworldly woman whose brother has promised to cure Cúchulainn of a strange wasting disease he has contracted after a dream in which two women beat him with flails. Emer and the women of the Ulaid drive off the woman who has entranced her husband and she goes on to lambast men in general for constantly lusting after other women.

The final act in the hero's life is, of course, the story of his death. In the fight against Medb of Connacht, described in the Tain, Cúchulainn kills Cailitin, whose wife, after his death, gives birth to three sons and three daughters. Medb sends these children to a wizard in Scotland to learn the dark arts and, when they come back, sets them against Cúchulainn. They go to Emain Macha and begin to make an Otherworldly noise, howling and screaming, so it sounds like the fortress is being attacked by a whole army.

Cúchulainn is ready to confront the danger, but Cathbad tells him to wait for three days before doing anything, by which time the trouble will all be over. He goes back to Emer and the other women of the Ulaid, including the beautiful Niamh, who all tell him he should stay with them.

One of the daughters of Cailitin, assuming the form of Niamh, tries to tempt Cúchulainn out of the fortress. He knows the end is near, that the prophecy of an early death is coming true, and Emer once again implores him to stay but, telling her he has never shirked a fight and that, if he dies, his fame will last forever, he leaves the fortress. Once outside, he meets three old crones, perhaps the daughters of Cailitin, and they are roasting a dog over a fire. One of them offers Cúchulainn, the Hound of Culann, some of the dog meat, catching him in a dilemma. To eat dog meat would be to break a *geis*, a taboo prohibiting such things, but to refuse the offer of hospitality would also be breaking another *geis*. At first he tries to get past the crones, until one taunts him, saying he is too high and mighty to eat with them. He accepts the offered shoulder blade of the dog and, holding it in his left hand, takes a bite, then hides the rest of it under his left leg. But it is too late and the *geis* takes hold, draining the strength out of the left side of his body.

Despite his weakened state, Cúchulainn continues on to the battle. Ranged against him are three sons of men he has killed and they have all been armed with spears by the sons of Cailitin. The first throws his spears and kills Láeg, Cúchulainn's charioteer, spilling his guts on the floor of the chariot. The second throws and hits one of Cúchulainn's horses, the Grey of Macha, and then Lugaid, the son of Cú

Roi, throws his spear. It penetrates Cúchulainn's armour and ruptures his intestines, which spill out of his body.

Cúchulainn tries to hold his stomach together and drags himself to a lake for a drink of water. As he drinks a raven drinks his blood and pecks at his intestines (in Celtic mythology lakes and birds are both associated with the Otherworld). He laughs at the raven and, not wanting to die on his stomach, ties himself to a rock so he can face his enemy on his feet. They don't have the courage to approach him for three days, until a bird lands on the rock near his head and his eyes don't flicker, so they know that the great hero is dead.

The Táin

The Táin, or to give its full title the *Táin Bo Cúailnge*, is the centrepiece of both the Ulster Cycle and of early Irish literature in general, as well as being one of the crucial works in Irish literary history. Some of the stories of Irish mythology are fragmentary and unsatisfying but this cannot be said of the Táin. The power of its language and the intensity of its imagery give it a place in world literature as an outstanding survival of the oral tradition, even if the versions of it that survive are far from perfect. The Irish American literary scholar James MacKillop sums it up in the following way:

> For wealth of detail, vividness of characterisation and enumeration of episode, not to mention sheer length, the *Táin Bo Cúailnge* can stand comparison with the national epics of Europe. It is not, however, a highly fin-

ished work. To begin with it lacks a unifying narrative tone. Successive episodes do not advance continuing themes. Scant motivation appears for abrupt shifts in character.[30]

In part, the faults identified by MacKillop stem from the episodic nature of the narrative, a result of the Táin's roots in the oral tradition, and from the fact that it does not exist in one authoritative manuscript edition. A full version of the narrative can only be assembled by combining parts taken from the available manuscripts, usually from what are known as Recension I and Recension II, and the quality of these is quite variable, relying as they do on the skill and perseverance of the different redactors. This can give the Táin the impression of being cobbled together, although the skill of the translators of modern English versions tends to minimise this effect. Despite such reservations, it would not be unreasonable to speak of the Táin in the same breath as *The Iliad*, another epic narrative of fierce combat and one of the greatest works in all world literature.

The title now in general use, the Táin, was the one adopted by the Irish poet Thomas Kinsella for his brilliant translation of 1969, which includes evocative illustrations by Louis de Brocquy, one of Ireland's foremost artists. The first part of the full name, *Táin Bo*, can be translated as 'cattle raid', although a more literal version would be 'the driving off of the cattle'. *Cúailnge* is the Old Irish name for the hilly piece of land that juts out into the Irish Sea in County Louth, just south of the border between the Irish Republic and Northern Ireland, now known as the Cooley Peninsula. Translations before Kinsella's version often rendered the title into English – 'The Cattle Raid of Cooley' or something similar – but opinion now firmly favours the Irish title, particularly since the Irish word 'Táin' can have other meanings than 'cattle raid', including a 'meeting' or 'collection of people'. Ciaran Carson, whose vibrant translation appeared in 2007, point outs that, bearing in mind the Táin was originally written on calf-skin vellum, it is possible to think of *Táin Bo Cúailnge* as having a dual meaning that includes a physical description of what it actually is, a collection of stories written on calf-skin.[31]

At its most basic, the plot of the Táin relates an attack by the armies of Connacht on Ulster with the purpose of stealing or, to be more precise, running off a particularly highly-prized bull. It can be seen as forming a sub-genre of stories concerning cattle raids within the Ulster Cycle, along with six other, shorter stories such as the *Táin Bo Fráich* and the *Táin Bo Flidais* (the cattle raids of Fráich and Flidais respectively). Such a concentration of stories on the same subject gives a good indication of the importance attached to the ownership of cattle in Ireland at that time, both in purely agricultural terms (cattle being valuable as sources of meat, milk and leather) and as status symbols in society. A wealthy person owned a large number of cows, a sign of power and prestige, and there can also be no doubt of the association of the bull with strength and virility. To own a great bull, one which had sired many calves, said a great deal about the owner, much as a man in the throes of a mid-life crisis might think owning a Ferrari does for him now.

The story itself gets off to a fairly low-key start with the episode of 'The Pillow Talk'. In some versions, including

Kinsella's translation, this is preceded by the *remscéla*, or pre-tales, a selection of other stories from the Ulster Cycle which give some context to the story and background to the characters appearing in it, although, it could be argued, these hold up the start of the real action. The inclusion of the *remscéla* may represent the practice of the oral story-tellers, who, it is thought, would have approached a performance of the Táin by setting the scene with some shorter, related stories. These could also have acted as a warm-up for the storyteller and the audience, getting both into the mood for what was to come.

At the start of the Táin proper, then, Medb, the Queen of Connacht, is in bed with Ailill, her consort, who is of lower rank than she is, and they are talking about how well-off they both are and comparing their possessions. Both have similar fortunes, but Ailill just about comes out on top because he owns the great white-horned bull Finnbennach, which has proved itself to be highly fertile. Medb is not best pleased about this and later, together with the Ulster exile Fergus mac Róich, also her lover, she comes up with a plan to acquire a bull in Ulster of which Fergus knows and which he considers to be at least the equal of Finnbennach. This bull is called Donn Cúailnge (the brown Bull of Cooley) and Medb sends word to its owner, saying she wants to borrow it for a year and offering, amongst other things, to sleep with the owner if that's what it takes to get what she wants, a ploy she will use on a number of occasions throughout the course of the Táin.

The owner of the Donn Cúailnge rejects Medb's advances after discovering she was planning to take the bull by force if necessary and she takes this rejection as a great insult to her honour. Together with Ailill, Medb decides to mount a cattle raid to get the bull and begins to assemble an army at her fortress, which includes warriors from Leinster and Fergus's 3,000 exiled Ulstermen, as well as her own soldiers from Connacht.

Before this great army sets out for Ulster, Medb consults Fedelm, a young female poet and seer, to ask what lies ahead. Fedelm does not prophesy success for Medb's proposed raid, responding to questions about what will happen by saying 'I see it crimson, I see it red'[32] She goes on to warn Medb about the danger posed by Cúchulainn, saying:

> Blood spurts from soldier's bodies
> released by this hero's hand.
> He kills on sight, some thing
> Dela's followers and clan [the warriors of Ireland]
> Women wail at the corpse-mound
> because of him – the Forge-Hound[33]

These dire warnings don't prevent Medb from setting out. She already knows of the curse afflicting the Ulaid, which has disabled them with what is described as pains like those experienced by women during childbirth. But Cúchulainn is not affected by the curse and, although at first distracted by an appointment with a woman, when he hears of the army approaching Ulster, he sets out to confront them on his own, hoping to delay them for long enough for the Ulaid to rise from their curse and repel the attack.

At first Cúchulainn doesn't engage directly with the approaching army. He leaves challenges, written in ogham, which they must accomplish before they can proceed. To go on without meeting the challenges would be to break a *geis* and risk the future good fortune of the entire expedition. But the men overcome each hurdle Cúchulainn puts in their way and advance further into Ulster territory. He adopts the tactics of guerrilla warfare, harassing the army whenever he can, picking off those warriors unwise enough to leave the main party and carrying out hit-and-run raids. Every night he mounts these raids on the enemy's camp, killing hundreds of soldiers at a time, but he can only delay the advance of the army, not stop it entirely. As the army approaches Cúailgne, Medb sends out a party of warriors charged with capturing the great bull, which can smell them coming and, with the shape-shifting goddess of war Morrigan on his shoulder in the form of a raven, carves great furrows out of the ground with his hooves in his anger.

The nightly killing raids are having a devastating effect on the morale of the army and Fergus goes to Cúchulainn at his camp to negotiate an agreement to limit the fighting to one single combat a day, each held at a ford in a river, the traditional spot for such fighting. There follows a long sequence of these fights, each at a different location, and the events of these fights give rise to the names by which these places will henceforth be known. The conduct of each fight between Cúchulainn and the warrior from Connacht's army is different but the outcome is always the same. Cúchulainn kills each opponent and, on most occasions, takes his head as a trophy. But, in the meantime, and despite Cúchulainn's best efforts to prevent it, Medb's soldiers succeed in running off Donn Cúailgne.

Morrigan then confronts Cúchulainn in many different forms. She appears as a raven and as a wolf, and she even takes on the form of an eel in order to twist around his legs, trying to trip him up. Cúchulainn's father Sualtam, who can be seen as the personification of the god Lugh, comes to help him, allowing him to sleep for three days and three nights to restore his strength and recover from his numerous wounds.

A band of boys from the Ulaid then arrive from Emain Macha, young trainee warriors who have not been affected by the curse because of their youth. They have come to Cúchulainn's aid while he is sleeping, taking up the fight with the army of Connacht. They each kill one warrior before being killed themselves and, of the 150 who came, only one is left at the end of the fight. Cúchulainn wakes from his sleep and, on learning of the death of the boys, flies into a war rage, a warp spasm in the words of Kinsella, and mounts a ferocious attack on his enemy's camp, circling it in his chariot and killing warriors with sling shot and spear. Hundreds more of Medb's army are killed and she decides to return to the former plan of only engaging in single combat. The only question is who will be the next warrior to face the Hound of Culann, who has slaughtered all those who have come up against him.

Medb decides the only warrior who is capable of beating Cúchulainn is Ferdiad, one of the exiled Ulstermen, who grew up with Cúchulainn and learned to fight with him, the two of them becoming as close as brothers. Medb tries to persuade Ferdiad to take up the challenge, offering him both herself and marriage to her daughter Finnabair as inducements, but Ferdiad is reluctant to go up against his friend. Then the warriors of the Connacht army tell Ferdiad he will be dishonoured if he refuses the challenge and he finally gives in and accepts.

Cúchulainn doesn't want to fight Ferdiad either, not because he is frightened, but because of the close bond of friendship between them. Nevertheless he meets Ferdiad at a ford at the appointed time. An epic battle begins between the two closely matched warriors but, even though they fight with all their strength, they abide by the rules of single combat, giving each other the choice of weapons at the beginning of each day and, after the fighting has finished at the end of the day, offering each other medical help and food.

On the fourth day of fighting Ferdiad drives his sword into Cúchulainn's chest and, at almost the same instant, Cúchulainn spikes Ferdiad on the end of his spear. Cúchulainn calls for his charioteer Láeg to bring the *gáe bolga*, a magical weapon like a spear which splinters into 30 barbs when it penetrates a body and can only be used under special circumstances. Kinsella describes what happens next in the following way:

Cúchulainn caught it (the *gáe bolga*) in the fork of his foot and sent it casting towards Ferdiad and it went through the deep and sturdy apron of twice-smelted iron, and shattered in three parts the stout strong stone the size of a mill-stone, and went coursing through the highways and byways of his body so that every single joint filled with barbs.

'That's enough now,' Ferdiad said, 'I'll die of that'.[34]

After Ferdiad dies, Cúchulainn laments the death of his friend and, weakened by his wounds, he cannot rise to the warnings from Láeg of the approaching Connacht army. Cethern, son of Fintan, comes to his aid, charging headlong into the warriors of Connacht and killing many but taking many wounds himself, arriving back at Cúchulainn's camp with 'his guts around his feet'. Healers come to attend to Cethern but, as each one successively tells him he will not survive, he kills them. Cúchulainn patches him up as best he can and Cethern, knowing he has not much longer to live, heads back into battle, inflicting great casualties on the enemy before his death.

After the death of Cethern, more warriors come to fight in place of Cúchulainn, both individually and in small groups, hurling themselves into battle until they have all been killed. Cúchulainn sends his father Sualtam to Emain Macha to rouse the rest of the Ulaid from their affliction but, when Sualtam gets there, he shouts out a warning immediately, breaking the *geis* of only speaking after the king has spoken. (The king, in his turn, can only speak after a druid.) Nobody will do anything to help Sualtam and he gets increasingly agitated until he falls over his shield, cutting his head off on its sharpened rim. The severed head continues to issue the warning and, finally, Conchobar pays attention. He issues the command for the men of Ulster to rise from their curse, pronouncing a long list of the names of people and places for his son to visit to convey the news. This is something of a challenge for the English reader, although in the original Irish the names would all have had meanings and associations for a contemporary audience. They would have functioned as a sort of sound map, picking out names from around Ulster which would lead the audience around the province in their minds as they picked up on the stories and happenings connected with the names.

The Ulster army assembles and goes out to meet the army of Connacht. Cúchulainn is still recovering from his wounds and can take no part in the action as the armies meet but, when word reaches him of an attempt by Fergus to capture Conchobar, he flies into a war rage. He heads into the fray looking for Fergus, who withdraws from the field rather than face Cúchulainn, taking the 3,000 Ulster exiles with him. Cúchulainn's arrival proves the turning point and, recognising Connacht are losing the battle, Medb sends Donn Cúailnge back to Connacht before leaving the field herself. Cúchulainn finds her relieving herself and tells her he has the right to kill her, but will not because he doesn't kill women.

The great bull arrives in Connacht and challenges Finnbennach. A huge fight erupts and the roaring and bellowing of the two bulls can be heard for miles around. They fight all night, throwing themselves into a lake from which, at dawn, Donn Cúailnge emerges with Finnbennach's entrails hanging from his horns. The Connacht army go to kill Donn Cúailnge, but Fergus stops them and the bull heads back to Ulster, leaving a trail of gore behind him. When he gets there, he dies. Ailill and Medb make peace with Ulster and Cúchulainn, and the story ends with the men of Ulster returning to Emain Macha in triumph.

The Fenian Cycle

The stories making up the Fenian Cycle, most of which concern the exploits of the other great hero of Irish mythology Fionn mac Cumhaill, should, perhaps, go under the heading of the Fianna Cycle. 'Fenian' is a nineteenth-century coinage, meaning something along the lines of 'old Irish'. However the word has now become so embedded in the English language, gaining its associations with Irish Republicanism as it has done so, that it would be almost impossible now to replace 'The Fenian Cycle' with something more appropriate.

The Fianna were bands of young men, mostly made of the landless nobility or those waiting for an inheritance, who were engaged in training in the arts of hunting and war. Stories of their exploits mostly survive from fifteenth-century manuscript collections, although the language used in the stories can be dated by linguistic methods to the twelfth century. The most important source is known as *Acallam Na Senórach*, usually translated into English as *The Colloquy of the Ancients* or *Tales of the Elders of Ireland*. The stories in this collection take the form of a dialogue between the last two surviving members of the Fianna, the ageing Caílte and Oisín, and St Patrick. This is obviously a literary device but does, at least, suggest the stories are set before St Patrick arrived in Ireland in the fifth century.

Stories concerning Fionn, often called Finn MacCool in English, have survived into the modern world to a much greater extent than stories from any of the other cycles. They have been told in one form or another in the folklore of Ireland, Scotland and the Isle of Man right up to present times. An example of their survival comes from the Scottish Gaelic community of Cape Breton in Nova Scotia, Canada, whose ancestors first came to the area as a result of the Highland Clearances of the eighteenth century. The Gaelic-speaking storyteller Joe Neil MacNeil, who died in 1997 at the age of 89, recounted many tales of the exploits of Fionn and the Fianna, taking them from his extensive repertoire of stories.[35] This is a testimony to their continuing popularity which is itself the most likely reason for their survival, as those that did not go down well with an audience would quickly get dropped. It is possible to think of these modern folktales as representing a living tradition of the Fenian Cycle. The storytellers do not necessarily recount the old stories as if they were set in stone, but have adapted them to the tastes of modern audiences and have also invented new ones to add to the canon.

The length of time the character of Fionn has been in circulation is one of the reasons depictions of him are far less consistent than Cúchulainn, who is always the hero and is always fighting. Fionn has changed a number of times and is not always shown in a favourable light, being sometimes devious and sometimes the fool. Dáithí Ó hÓgáin thinks Fionn is actually a composite character, the conflation of a number of different mythological types. He sees the origins of the character developing out of the cult of the seer in Leinster at an early date, well before the fifth century, placing it within the Druidic tradition.[36] He goes on to suggest that Fionn became associated with the struggle between Leinster and the Ui Néill clan over possession of the Boyne Valley in the fifth and sixth centuries, with Fionn being portrayed as a war leader as well as a seer. This would eventually lead to him becoming associated with the Fianna.

One of the best known stories in the cycle is 'The Boyhood Deeds of Fionn' (*Macgnímartha Finn*). The story starts by recounting how Cumhaill, Fionn's father, dies at the hands of Goll mac Morna, who will go on to become a leader of the Fianna and Fionn's rival in a number of other stories. In a later episode, Fionn is studying under the tutelage of the druid Finnegas, who has been trying to catch a magical fish, the Salmon of Knowledge, for many years. The salmon will give the person who eats it all of the knowledge in the world and Finnegas, after finally catching it, cooks it over a fire, telling Fionn not to eat it as he wants to keep the knowledge for himself. But Fionn cannot resist touching the fish and, in doing so, burns his thumb, which he sticks in his mouth to soothe the pain. Fionn gains the knowledge because of this, at the expense of the druid, and, from then on, whenever he wants to have access to this knowledge, in the form of prophecies, all he has to do is suck his thumb.

Another of the well known stories is 'The Pursuit of Diarmuid and Gráinne' (*Tóraigheacht Dhiarmada agus Ghráinne*). It concerns a love triangle between Fionn, here depicted as an old king, and the young lovers Diarmuid and Gráinne, similar to the one in the story of Naoise and Deirdre from the Ulster Cycle. Fionn is mourning the death of his wife and the Fianna decide to find another woman to take her place. They choose Gráinne, who initially agrees, but is shocked to find when she meets Fionn that he is older than her father. At the feast to celebrate the betrothal, she sees Diarmuid, a handsome young member of the Fianna, and immediately falls in love with him. She slips a sleeping draught to all the other guests at the feast and, while they are asleep, attempts to persuade Diarmuid to run away with her. At first he stays loyal to Fionn, but soon changes his mind and the couple flee to the forest.

Fionn wakes up and, along with the Fianna, pursues the runaway couple. He soon catches up with them and wants vengeance, but his son Oisín, along with Diarmuid's other friends in the Fianna, persuade him not to do anything rash. Diarmuid and Gráinne escape with the help of his friends and Angus Óg, the god of love and poetry, and they are chased by Fionn all over Ireland and Scotland.

During the pursuit Diarmuid at first refuses to sleep with Gráinne, because of his respect for Fionn and, when they are crossing a stream where water splashes on Gráinne's leg, she tells him the water has more daring than he has. It does not take long for Diarmuid's passion to get the better of his respect for Fionn and Gráinne becomes pregnant. She develops a craving for rowan berries from a tree guarded by the one-eyed giant Searbhán, who refuses to give any of the berries to the lovers. Diarmuid fights the giant, who initially protects himself with magic, but is overcome when Diarmuid learns how to turn the giant's own iron club against him. Diarmuid climbs into the tree to pick the sweetest berries from the top branches and, while he is there, Fionn and the Fianna arrive, sitting down under the tree to a game of *fidcell*, a board game similar to chess. Fionn plays Oisín and, with Diarmuid watching the game from above, begins to get the better of his son. Diarmuid helps Oisín by throwing berries onto the squares to indicate a move, but it is not long before Fionn realises what is happening and demands that Diarmuid show himself. Diarmuid and Gráinne kiss three times before Angus Óg spirits her away. Diarmuid climbs down from the tree and escapes from Fionn again by jumping over the heads of the assembled Fianna.

The couple go on to live together in a place where Fionn cannot touch them and Angus Óg negotiates a peace between all parties. Some years later, when Diarmuid and Gráinne have had five children, Fionn organises a boar hunt near where they live and Diarmuid agrees to join the hunting party, despite knowing he will be breaking a *geis* by hunting boar. During the hunt Diarmuid is gored by a boar as he is in the process of killing it and Fionn gloats over his prostrate body. Diarmuid tells him that he has the power to heal the wounds if he lets the younger man drink water out of his hands. Fionn goes to a well twice to get water in his hands and, on both occasions, lets it slip through his fingers before Diarmuid has had a chance to drink. Oscar, Fionn's grandson, threatens to attack him if he does it again and Fionn goes to the well a third time, but, when he gets back, it is too late. Diarmuid has died.

This story shows Fionn in a dark light, prepared to let a young man die out of jealousy. In many later stories his character is much lighter. He is the butt of jokes or is forced to undergo mock heroic trials, like having to whistle while he is eating oatmeal, which has predictable results. Later still, in folktales, he has transformed into whatever the storyteller requires him to be. In a well known tale, which does not appear to go back more than a few centuries, Fionn, now called Finn MacCool, is credited with building the Giant's Causeway, the unusual rock formation that juts out into the Atlantic Ocean in County

Antrim, Northern Ireland. The causeway is supposed to cross the sea to the Scottish island of Staffa, where there is a similar rock formation called Fingal's Cave, Fingal being a Scottish version of Fionn's name. Fionn built the causeway so he could walk to Scotland to fight another giant but, in one version of the story, he falls asleep before setting out and the Scottish giant comes looking for him. The Scottish giant is much bigger than Fionn and he is terrified, but his wife comes to the rescue. She dresses Fionn up in baby clothes and, when the Scottish giant arrives and sees the size of what he thinks is Fionn's baby son, he loses his nerve at the thought of how big the father must be and runs away back to Scotland, tearing up the causeway behind him as he goes.

The Mythological Cycle

The gods and goddess of pre-Christian Ireland have a mostly hidden presence in many of the stories making up the canon of mythology, cropping up in what is known as a euhemerised form. In other words, they have been changed in the stories into mortal form and appear as heroes and kings. This is the case in stories in all of the cycles, and one of the main reasons why they can be regarded as making up a mythology, but it is particularly true of the stories of the so-called Mythological Cycle, where the deities of the pre-Christian Irish pantheon come closest to the surface.

One of the main sources of these stories is *The Book of Invasions* (*Lebor Gabála Erenn*, literally 'The Book of the Taking of Ireland'), already mentioned in Chapter 2, a copy of which is contained in the eleventh-century manuscript volume *The Book of Leinster*. *The Book of Invasions* is made up of a miscellaneous collection of stories and poetry and is sometimes described as being a pseudo-history because the intention of the redactors appears to have been to trace the history of the Irish people by constructing a more or less continuous sequence of events out of mythical stories, Biblical sources, bardic poetry and just about anything else available which fitted the purpose. Many of the events recounted are linked to the Old Testament. Characters from the Irish stories are related to Biblical characters, through suggestions that they are, for example, descendants of Noah or members of the Lost Tribe of Israel. The overall purpose would appear to be to create a narrative of the origins of the Irish similar to the Old Testament account of the Israelites. How seriously this was taken as a historical work is hard to say, but the result has been to preserve mythological stories within a framework of what purports to be a work of Christian scholarship.

What *The Book of Invasions* does not do is contain any Irish mythological creation stories, giving an account of the origins of the universe as the pre-Christian religion would have described it. Assuming such stories once existed, they would have served a comparable purpose to the opening verses of Genesis in the Bible, with its opening line, 'In the beginning God created the heavens and the earth'. The history of the Irish people given in *The Book of Invasions* dates back to the Biblical flood, after which the country was occupied by the Scoti, people who arrived in Ireland, according to the book, from ancient Scythia.

Ireland was subjected to a succession of six invasions,

the first five of which were by divine or semi-divine beings known by the names of their leaders. The first invasion was that of the Cesair, and they were followed by the Partholonians, the Nemedians, the Fir Bolg and the Tuatha Dé Danaan (literally the people of the goddess Danu). Throughout this time, battles occur against the Fomorians, a band of semi-divine raiders from the sea, and it is one of these battles which provides the basis for one of the best known stories from the cycle, 'The Second Battle of Mag Tuired' (*Cath Tánaiste Maige Tuired*). In the story, the Tuatha Dé Danaan battle against the oppression of the Fomorians to regain control of Ireland. The main action involves the Tuatha Dé Danaan leader Lug Lámfhota (Lug of the Long Arm, who is obviously based on the god Lugh) and his fight against his grandfather Balor of the Evil Eye and his half-brother, the devious and cowardly Bres. The battle is long and bloody, with many casualties on both sides, until Lug wins the fight by using a slingshot to throw a stone straight into Balor's single eye. The stone goes right through Balor's skull and, as well as killing him, kills all the Formorians behind him.

The final invasion sees the Milesians, a mortal people named after Míl Espáine, the man who originally led them to Spain, take on the Tuatha Dé. The descendants of Mil invade Ireland from their base in Spain (as already mentioned in Chapter 2), taking over the country after a series of battles. Later stories say that, after the Tuatha Dé lost the land to the Milesians, who are the ancestors of the modern Irish, they descended underground to live within the earthen mounds called *sidhe* which dot the Irish landscape, where, if the stories are to be believed, they remain to this day.

Other popular stories from the cycle include 'The Children of Lir' (*Leannaí Lir*), in which the four children of a king are transformed into swans for 900 years, 'The Wooing of Étain' (*Tochmarc Étaíne*), a story of the beautiful Étain sometimes placed in the Ulster cycle, and 'The Vision of Angus Óg' (*Aislinge Óenguso*). This last story is a romantic tale in which Angus Óg falls in love with a beautiful girl he sees in his dreams. He becomes sick with love and goes in search of the girl, until he sees her in the midst of a crowd of 150 other girls. He finds out that her name is Caer, but he cannot get to meet her. Some time later he goes to the shore of a lake, where he is told she will be, and sees a flock of 150 swans on the water. He calls out her name and one of the swans comes towards him. He recognises the swan as the girl he loves. In order to be with her, he transforms into a swan himself and they fly off together.

The Cycles of the Kings

The Cycles of the Kings is a more recent categorisation of a group of stories than the other three cycles. The term was coined by the Irish literary critic Myles Dillon in 1946, who used it to define stories dealing with early kings of Ireland. Some of these kings are entirely mythological, while some have elements of mythology and history combined together and others are definitely historical. Brian Boru, for example, falls into this last category, ruling Ireland from 1002 to 1014, although this does not necessarily mean the stories about him are entirely accurate.

The stories were conceived by court poets, the *filid*, who, as part of their duties, composed poetry and prose concerning the genealogies of their patrons. Needless to say, the main purpose of these stories was the aggrandisement of whichever member of the nobility they were intended for, who was generally shown to have descended from a line of heroic ancestors. In order to achieve this heroic ancestry, the poet might mix elements of mythology with history, known genealogy and whatever else came to hand. As a consequence these stories are entirely unreliable as historical documents.

The cycles have been described as being less heroic than the Ulster Cycle, less romantic than the Fenian Cycle and less magical than the Mythological Cycle and, while there is an element of truth in this, some of the stories are not without merit. One of the few to have had much of an impact on a modern audience is 'The Madness of Sweeney' (*Buile Suibhne*), which concerns Suibhne, now often written as Sweeney, the king of Dál nAraide, an area of northern Ireland now mostly in County Antrim. In the story, the king becomes annoyed at the constant ringing of bells in the church being built by St Ronan and storms out of his house to make his feelings on the subject known. In his haste, and because his wife tries to stop him doing anything rash by refusing to give him his coat, the king goes to Ronan naked and, in the ensuing scuffle, throws Ronan's psalter into a lake. Before anything more drastic can happen, Suibhne is called away to fight in a battle and Ronan, apparently not a man to bear a grudge, accompanies him to bless the soldiers going into battle. Suibhne is not having this and throws a spear at Ronan, missing him but killing one of his aides. Another spear also misses Ronan and this one hits the church bell and breaks it. Ronan's patience is now exhausted and he curses Suibhne. By the curse, Suibhne is condemned to madness every time he hears a sharp sound like that of a bell and to die at the point of a spear.

Suibhne's madness causes him to become like a bird, terrified of people and hopping from foot to foot. He flees from the company of men to wander through Ireland and live in the wild, perching in trees to sleep at night. Eventually he is taken in at a monastery, where he is fed by a woman. Her husband, on hearing of this, runs Suibhne through with a spear. Suibhne then confesses his sins to a priest and is given the last rites before he dies and is finally released from his torment.

The story mixes mythological symbolism, of birds and lakes, with the Christian message of redemption. It has influenced a number of modern writers, including Flann O'Brien, who incorporated much of the story into his comic masterpiece *At Swim-Two-Birds*. The Nobel Prize-winning poet Seamus Heaney has translated the story under the title *Sweeney Astray*. It was published in 1984 to critical acclaim and has become the version of the story now most often read.

Adventures and Voyages

A number of the stories contained in the manuscripts don't fit conveniently into any of the cycles. These are generally known by the Old Irish words *Echtrae*, which means 'adventures', and *Immrama*, meaning 'voyages'. Notable examples are 'The Voyage of Bran' (*Immrama Bran*) and 'The Voyage of Máel Dúin' (*Immrama Máel Dúin*). Characteristically these stories involve a voyage into the Otherworld, which may be across the sea or underground. The main difference between the two genres is that, in the adventures, the stories relate the events actually occurring in the Otherworld, while, in the voyages, the narrative concentrates on what happens on the journey to the Otherworld. There are obvious parallels between these stories and the later tale of The Voyage of St Brendan, in which the saint sets out in a curragh, a traditional Irish boat, in search of the Isle of the Blessed, identified by some as America.

Tales from Wales

The Mabinogion

In all likelihood, the storytelling tradition in Wales was as strong as it was in Ireland, but far fewer of these stories have survived and those that do are in manuscripts of a considerably later date than the Irish equivalents. The main corpus is made up of the stories of the Mabinogion, which come from two fourteenth-century manuscripts. *The Red Book of Hergest* (*Llyfr Coch Hergest*), now held in the Bodleian Library in Oxford, has been dated to the late fourteenth century. The name simply derives from its red leather binding and its association with Hergest Court in Herefordshire, although the book is thought to be originally from South Wales. The other manuscript collection is slightly older, dating to about 1350, and is known as *The White Book of Rhydderch*. It appears to have been compiled by scribes in the Cistercian abbey of Strata Florida, the ruins of which are near Tregaron in mid-Wales, and it is now in the National Library of Wales in Aberystwyth.

The stories were given their collective name by Lady Charlotte Guest, who published translations in the 1830s and 1840s. Mabinogion appears to have been a scribal error in one of the manuscripts, but was assumed to be the plural form of *mabinogi* by Lady Guest and now both versions are in use, the form employed depending more on the preference of the individual using it than anything else. Various theories have been put forward as to the meaning of the word. Some suggest it denotes stories concerning the goddess Mabon, while others say it translates to 'Stories of Youth'. Current scholarly opinion sees the word as one simply used by the scribes to indicate that they were writing a story rather than a poem or a piece of history.

Lady Guest included twelve stories in her collection, although one of these, 'The Tale of Taliesin', is of a much later date than the other eleven and does not come from either of the two manuscripts, so it is not usually included in modern collections. Four of the stories form a distinct group, known as 'The Four Branches of the Mabinogi', while the other seven are not put together in any particular order in the manuscripts. Despite this they are generally split into two groups: 'The Three Romances', comprising tales with Arthurian content, and 'The Native Tales', which are really just the remaining four stories lumped together for the sake of convenience.

Putting a date on the original composition of the stories is problematic, as it is for the Irish stories and any others arising from an oral tradition. Influences of pre-Christian mythology are certainly there, but so are those of the later Christian period, as well as clear parallels with the medieval European romance tradition of storytelling. The lack of clear dates makes it difficult to say, among other things, if the Welsh stories influenced the Arthurian romances of Chrétien de Troyes, written in France towards the end of the twelfth century, or if the influence came in the other direction, with the Arthurian elements being incorporated into the Welsh stories as a result of Anglo-Norman incursions into Wales after the Norman Conquest of England in 1066. A further possibility, of both sets of stories being based on the same source of an older date which has been lost, is an attractive idea, as it suggests the Arthur stories existed in a pre-Christian cycle similar to those of Ireland, but there is no direct evidence for such an assertion.

The final victory of the English over the Welsh was not until 1282 and for much of the early medieval period before this Wales was not a single political entity, being made up of four main kingdoms, Gwynedd, Powys, Deheubarth and Morgannwg, roughly equivalent to the areas we now think of as North Wales, Mid Wales, West Wales and South Wales. These separate kingdoms were, themselves, rarely ruled by a single king, but were divided among various princes and noble families. This was a period of conflicts between rival claimants to the thrones, shifting alliances both between rival families and within them, and warfare between kingdoms. It is against this background, of constant threat and regular fighting, that the stories of the Mabinogion are set.

The content of the stories is quite variable and attempts have been made to compare it to the Irish tradition, although, in general, the differences between the two are more obvious than the similarities. Some of the names used in the two traditions certainly appear to have shared roots – the Welsh god and goddess Ludd and Dôn seem to be linked to the Irish Lugh and Danu – but the way in which these deities are portrayed in human form doesn't necessarily suggest they were perceived in the same way on either side of the Irish Sea. The Irish and Welsh languages are thought to have diverged from each other by the first millennium BC and it is tempting to envisage a single source for both mythologies going back to a proto-Celtic language in existence before the split. Unfortunately, the surviving texts in either language simply do not provide enough evidence to be able to say for certain that this was the case.

The following section deals exclusively with the stories of 'The Four Branches of the Mabinogi'. This is not to say the other stories of the Mabinogion are without merit, but rather that these four stories are the best known and can stand as examples of the tradition in general.

The Four Branches

The relationships between 'The Four Branches' are apparent, but they do not by any means form a continuous narrative. A number of characters crop up in different stories but only one, Pryderi, son of Pwyll and Rhiannon, is in all four, although he is not a major character in the first two. The Four Branches could represent the surviving stories of a much larger cycle concerning the life and exploits of Pryderi, although it is just as likely the name was adopted by later redactors of the story as a means of linking the branches together. As with much to do with the origins of the Mabinogion, it is possible to speculate, but not to know for certain.

No names are given for the stories in the manuscripts. Most of them end with a line along the lines of 'Here ends this branch of the Mabinogi', so they are now either known as a branch of the Mabinogi or by the name of the main character in each story. The First Branch is sometimes called 'Pwyll, Prince of Dyfed' because it relates two episodes in his life. In the first part of the story Pwyll is out hunting with his hounds when he hears another pack of hounds in the distance. He goes to see what is happening and finds that the hounds, which all have white bodies and red ears, showing they come from the Otherworld, have brought down a stag. Pwyll drives these hounds away and feeds his own dogs on the meat, but the owner of the other hounds arrives, riding a grey horse and dressed all in grey, and he is outraged by this discourtesy. Pwyll tells the man he would like to redeem himself, but needs to know who the man is in order to do so properly. The man introduces himself as Arawn, king of Annwfn, the Otherworld, and tells Pwyll he can redeem himself by ridding him of the oppression of Hafgan, a rival king. To do this Pwyll must change places with Arawn by taking on his appearance and ruling in his place for a year, at which point he can fight Hafgan who, because a second blow would only bring him back to life, can only be killed by a single blow from a sword.

So the two swap forms and Pwyll goes to Annwfn to rule in Arawn's place for a year. He proves himself to be a wise and just king and, at night, he sleeps in the same bed as Arawn's wife but turns his face to the wall without touching her. After the year has passed he meets Hafgan at the ford appointed as the place for the fight and, after a great battle, he manages to kill him with a single blow. Pwyll and Arawn return to their own lands and Arawn learns that Pwyll has both been a good leader and has not touched his wife. He realises that Pwyll has been a steadfast friend and the two of them remain on good terms, exchanging gifts of horses and hawks.

As it enters its second part, the story now changes abruptly. Pwyll is sitting on a mound near his fort because he has been told something bad or something wonderful will happen if he does. A beautiful woman slowly rides past the mound on a snow white horse (it has been suggested by some commentators that this represents the Celtic horse god Epona) and Pwyll wants to know who she he is. He sends a runner after her, but the runner cannot catch up with the white horse. Pwyll sends a rider on a fast horse, who also cannot catch up with the white horse even though the latter appears to be going so slowly. The next day Pwyll comes to the mound again and, when the white horse appears, sends a rider on the fastest horse he has after it, but the faster the rider chases the white horse the further away it appears to become. On the third day he goes after the white horse himself, but gets no closer, so he calls out for the woman to wait for him. She replies that she will be happy to wait for him and wishes he had asked earlier because it would have spared the horses.

Finally Pwyll meets the woman on the white horse and asks her who she is and what she is doing. She tells him she is Rhiannon and she has come to see him because she has been betrothed by her father to Gwawl, a man she does not love. A feast has been prepared and she invites Pwyll to come, which means, without actually saying it, that she is going to marry him. Once there, he meets a man he doesn't know who asks to be granted a favour. Pwyll agrees and Rhiannon tells him he has been stupid because the man is actually Gwawl, who asks him not to sleep with Rhiannon that night and to give him all the provisions prepared for the feast. Pwyll has to agree because he has already promised he would, even though he has, in effect, agreed to allow Gwawl to marry Rhiannon. She now says she will not marry Gwawl for another year and, after Gwawl has left, she gives Pwyll a special bag for the provisions of the feast that will take place then.

Gwawl comes back a year latter for the wedding and Pwyll's men try to fill the bag with provisions for the wedding feast, but, despite their best efforts, the provisions never reach the top of the bag. Gwawl is tricked into getting into the bag himself to tread the provisions down and, when he does, Pwyll closes the bag on top of him. He and his men then play a game called Badger in the Bag, in which each man takes it in turns to beat the bag. To stop the game and save his life, Gwawl gives his word that he will not take vengeance on anybody who has beaten him. He leaves the court and Pwyll and Rhiannon sit down to the feast together.

The couple go back to Dyfed when the feast is over and, after a long period without becoming pregnant, Rhiannon gives birth to a son, who goes missing the day after he is born. To avoid getting the blame themselves, Rhiannon's attendants kill some newly born pups and smear the sleeping Rhiannon's face and hands with their blood to make it look as if she has killed her son. Pwyll refuses to divorce Rhiannon, but comes up with a strange punishment for her. For the next seven years she must tell the story of how her son disappeared to everyone who comes to the castle and then offer to carry them on her back as if she were a horse.

In another part of Wales, an infant boy mysteriously appears in the stables of a lord, from where a newly born fowl has just disappeared. The lord and his wife, who are childless themselves, raise the boy as their own, calling him Gwri Wallt Euryn, Gwri of the Yellow Hair. As he gets older, his resemblance to Pwyll becomes unmistakeable and the couple decide they must return the boy to Pwyll's castle. The lord takes him and, when they arrive at the castle, Rhiannon tells the lord her story and offers him a ride on her back. He refuses her offer and takes the boy to Pwyll, saying he has brought the missing boy back. There is much rejoicing at the news and Rhiannon is released from her punishment. The story ends by saying that the boy was renamed as Pryderi and, after Pwyll has died, he goes on to rule the land as his heir.

In The Second Branch, also known as 'Branwen, Daughter of Llŷr', the Irish king Matholwch comes to Harlech to ask for Branwen's hand in marriage. Her brother Bendigeidfran, who is the king, agrees and a great feast begins, but her half-brother Efnysien is angry because he has not been consulted. To show his anger, he mutilates the horses owned by Matholwch by, amongst other things, cutting off their eyelids and ears. It is a great insult to Matholwch and Bendigeidfran tries to make amends by replacing the horses with some of his own and offering Matholwch gold and silver. He accepts, but Bendigeidfran can tell he is still not happy, so gives him a cauldron which has the power to restore the dead back to life.

Matholwch goes back to Ireland with Branwen, happy

that the insult has been put right and Branwen gives birth to a boy, whom they name Gwern. But the men of Ireland are not happy because they think the insult has not been avenged, so they send Branwen to the kitchen to cook for the court. While she is there, the butcher who delivers meat to the kitchen every day, boxes her around the ears.

The punishment and bullying continue for three years and, while it is going on, Branwen trains a starling to carry a message to Bendigeidfran, who, when he hears what is happening to his sister, assembles an army to invade Ireland. The army crosses the Irish Sea in boats, all except Bendigeidfran, who is so huge he wades across. The Irishmen see him coming and retreat across a river, destroying the bridge behind them. Bendigeidfran makes himself into a human bridge and his army cross the river by climbing over him. The Irish try to negotiate a peace by offering to build a house big enough for Bendigeidfran, an offer he accepts. Efnysien smells a rat and, when the house has been built, enters it first to check it out. He finds the Irish have tied hide bags to each of the pillars in the house and he asks what is in them. When they reply that it is only flour, he goes to one and sees there is an armed man hiding within it. He squeezes the bag, crushing the man's head, and goes to all the other bags and does the same.

The men of both countries enter the house from different ends and sit down together for a feast. All is going well until Efnysien again feels he has been insulted, this time by Matholwch's young son Gwern. He picks the boy up and throws him in the fire, sparking a huge fight between all the Irish and Welsh men. The corpses of the dead build up and the Irish begin to get the upper hand, as they throw their dead into the cauldron, bringing them back to life to carry on the fight. Efnysien sees what is happening and hides among the Irish dead, playing dead himself. He is thrown into the cauldron and, using all his strength, breaks it into pieces, bursting his own heart with the effort.

The slaughter continues, with even the women and children being killed, until there is nobody left alive in the whole of Ireland except for seven of the Welshmen, Branwen and Bendigeidfran, who has been fatally wounded in the foot by a poisoned spear. He orders the men to cut his head off and take it back to Harlech with them and, as they do so, the severed head continues to talk. Branwen also returns to Wales, but she is grief-stricken at the deaths of so many men and dies, wishing she had never been born at all. The men embark on a great feast, which goes on for years, and, back in Ireland, five pregnant women, it turns out, have survived the fighting by hiding in remote caves and their children go on to repopulate the country.

Pryderi is one of the seven Welshmen to have survived the slaughter in Ireland and, at the start of The Third Branch, 'Manawydan, Son of Llŷr', he goes back to his wife, Cigfa, in Dyfed, where he realises that Manawydan, Bendigeidfran's brother and heir, is alone in the world. Pryderi offers Manawydan the hand of his mother Rhiannon in marriage and, when the two of them meet, they instantly form a union. The two couples live happily in Dyfed, until one night a blanket mist descends across the whole county and, when it lifts, all the other people in Dyfed and all the domestic animals have disappeared.

At first the two couples survive by hunting and then, as the game gets scarce, they move to Hereford in England to start up a business making sandals. They become so successful, making such high quality goods, that the local craftsmen are all going out of business. They decide to protect their livelihoods by killing Pryderi and Manawydan, but the two Welshmen get to hear of their plans. The impulsive Pryderi wants to stay and fight, while the more cautious Manawydan advises discretion, saying they should move to another town. They go to another town, where they begin to make shields, but the pattern repeats itself and they move to yet another town, where they make shoes. After being driven out of the third town, they go back to Dyfed and live by hunting again.

On one of the hunts, Pryderi encounters a gleaming white boar, clearly an animal of the Otherworld. He chases it into a fort and, despite Manawydan's warning, follows it in through the gate. Manawydan waits outside until he is sure Pryderi is not coming out and returns to Rhiannon. She is not impressed with her husband for leaving her son behind and goes to the fort herself to find out what has happened. Inside she finds Pryderi gripping a bowl with both hands and unable to speak and she takes hold of the bowl herself, with the same consequences. The mist returns, blanking out everything, and when it lifts the fort, with Pryderi and Rhiannon inside it, has disappeared.

Manawydan and Cigfa are left alone in Dyfed and live as a chaste couple. After another unsuccessful trip to England, they return and sow three fields with wheat. A fine crop grows but, on the morning when Manawydan intends to harvest the wheat, he arrives at the fields to find a huge army of mice destroying the crop. He tries to stop them, but they are too quick for him. They escape easily from his grasp, all except for a particularly fat mouse, which he catches and puts into a glove.

The following day Manawydan decides to hang the mouse as punishment for the crime of theft and takes it to the same mound where Pwyll was sitting when he first saw Rhiannon. Before he has chance to hang the mouse, three strangers – a scholar, a priest and a bishop – appear, one after the other. These are the first strangers to have been seen in Dyfed since the first mist and each in turn asks Manawydan what he is doing with the mouse. He tells them he is executing it for stealing his wheat and each offers him increasingly large amounts of money for the mouse to stop him from doing something which, they say, they consider beneath him. He refuses each offer and the bishop asks him what he would accept for the mouse if he won't accept money, telling him to name his price. He says he wants Pryderi and Rhiannon to be returned and for the enchantment on the land brought by the fog to be lifted. The bishop agrees to the terms, but Manawydan still won't give him the mouse. He asks who the mouse really is and the bishop tells him it is his wife. He goes on to say that he is really Llwyd, son of Cil Coed, and that he is responsible for the enchantment on Dyfed, which he brought down in revenge for what happened to his friend Gwawl at the hands of Pwyll (in The First Branch). Before finally letting the mouse go, Manawydan asks Llwyd to promise not to cast any more spells on Dyfed and, when he agrees, gives him the mouse. It immediately transforms into Llwyd's wife, the land of Dyfed is restored to its former glory and Pryderi and Rhiannon are released.

The final story, The Fourth Branch, concerns Math, son

of Mathonwy, whose rule in Gwynedd coincides with Pryderi's rule in Dyfed. Rather bizarrely, he can only continue to live by keeping his feet in the lap of a virgin, unless he is at war, although no reason is given as to why this should be the case. Math's nephew Gilfaethwy falls in love with Goewin, the virgin. His brother Gwydion, a magician, comes up with a complicated plot to free Goewin from Math, involving tricking Pryderi into trading his pigs, animals new to Wales at the time, for horses and dogs conjured up by Gwydion. Pryderi realises he has been tricked and goes to war with Gwynedd. While Math is away at the fighting, Gilfaethwy forces himself on Goewin and rapes her so, when Math returns, he can no longer rest his feet in her lap. He is outraged and banishes his two nephews for three years, during which time they are transformed successively into male and female deer, then pigs and finally wolves. In each of these changed forms, they have one offspring, a fawn called Hyddwn, a piglet called Hychdwn Hir and the wolf cub Bleiddwn.

At the end of the three years the brothers are fully restored to themselves and to Math's court. Math asks Gwydion to advise him on who should be the next virgin and he recommends his sister Aranrhod. Math decides to test her, to see if she is really a virgin and, during the test, she gives birth to two boys and runs from the court in shame. One of the boys is called Dylan and he can swim as well as any fish, soon leaving the court to live in the sea. The other boy is brought up by Gwydion and remains unnamed for four years. Gwydion takes the boy to see Aranrhod, angering her because she remembers her shame, and she tells the boy he can only receive a name from her.

The trickster Gwydion comes up with a plan. He and the boy go to Aranrhod disguised as shoemakers so she doesn't recognise her son. She watches the boy throw a stone at a bird with such skill and accuracy that she calls him Lleu Llaw Gyffes, 'the fair-haired one of the skilful hand'. He is revealed as her son and she tells him he can never take up arms unless she gives him weapons first. Gwydion and Lleu now disguise themselves as bards and convince Aranrhod that her estate is coming under attack. She gives arms to Lleu, only to find she has been tricked again, so she tells Lleu he cannot have a wife from any race of people on earth.

Math and Gwydion together conjure up a beautiful young woman from the flowers of oak, broom and meadowsweet and call her Blodeuedd, meaning face of flowers, but also being the name for an owl. A feast is held, at which Lleu and Blodeuedd fall for each other and sleep together. Afterwards, Math gives them an estate in Dinoding, where they go to live. One day Lleu goes away to meet Math, leaving Blodeuedd on her own. She sees a hunter, Gronw Pebr, walking past the house and, as is customary, invites him in for refreshment. They immediately fall madly in love and sleep together that night. The next morning they devise a plan to get rid of Lleu so they can stay together. Blodeuedd must ask Lleu, who is all but invulnerable, how he can be killed, making out she is doing so because she is concerned for his safety. When she does this, Lleu tells her he can be killed by a thrust from a special spear, one made only on Sundays over the course of a year, and then only if it hits him while he has one foot in a bath of water and the other foot touching a billy goat.

Gronw and Blodeuedd contrive a situation where these conditions for Lleu's death can be met. Gronw throws the special spear at Lleu while he is getting out of a bath, besides which they have placed a goat. The spear hits Lleu, wounding him, but he escapes death by transforming into an eagle and flying away. With Lleu gone, Gronw takes his possessions and moves in with Blodeuedd. Gwydion, meanwhile, tracks down the eagle and changes Lleu back into human form. He also finds Blodeuedd, turning her into an owl and condemning her to never show her face during daylight again. Gronw offers to compensate Lleu for the injury and affront he has caused, but Lleu wants to return the blow he received. Gronw hides behind a stone, but Lleu throws his spear with such force it goes straight through the stone and kills him, allowing Lleu to regain his possessions. And, with that, 'The Four Branches of the Mabinogi' comes to an end.

Other Sources

The eleven stories of *The Mabinogion* provide the bulk of the surviving material relating to Welsh mythology, altered as they are in the medieval form in which we have them, but there are a number of other sources. These include the surviving examples of bardic poetry, which contain some allusions to mythology, and some pseudo-histories.

The Book of Taliesin is a fourteenth-century manuscript containing poetry of a much older date, attributed to the bardic poet Taliesin, who is traditionally said to have been working in the sixth century. There is no way of knowing if this is accurate, or even if Taliesin existed at all but, if true, it would make these poems some of the earliest written in the Welsh language. The collection includes 'The Battle of the Trees' (*Cad Goddeu*), a poem about a fight between Gwydion and Arawn, the king of the Otherworld, in which Gwydion enlists the trees of a forest to fight on his side.

Another manuscript, *The Book of Aneirin*, contains perhaps the best known of these poems, *Y Gododdin*, a series of elegies for the warriors of Gododdin, an area encompassing land on either side of the border between England and Scotland, who fell at what is thought to have been the Battle of Catterick, fought in about AD 600.

A collection of fragments, known as The Welsh Triads, exists in a number of manuscripts, including *The Red Book of Hergest* and *The White Book of Rhydderch*. These take the form of a list of three names, sometimes accompanied by an explanation of the story relating to the names and sometimes just as the names on their own. They appear to have been written down as a form of memory aid for the bardic poets and now provide an enigmatic glimpse of the range of stories a bard might have had at his disposal. The triads are often accompanied in the manuscripts by what is known as 'The Thirteen Treasures of the Island of Britain', a list of mostly magical items, such as White-Hilt, the Sword of Rhydderch Hael, which burst into flame when drawn, although the flames would not burn a worthy man.

Of the pseudo-histories, the best known is *The History of the Kings of Britain* by Geoffrey of Monmouth. It was written in about 1136 and claims to chronicle something like 2,000 years of British history, going back to the first king, who Geoffrey says was Brutus, the grandson of Aeneas from Troy, and includes accounts of King Lear and King

Arthur. As a work of historical scholarship *The History of the Kings of Britain* has serious limitations, not least Geoffrey's tendency towards fiction, but it retains an interest today because the author makes use of source material now lost.

And the Rest

Mythology and Folktales

So far this book has been considering Celtic mythology almost exclusively from an Irish and Welsh perspective. In this final chapter, the focus shifts on to the rest of what we now think of as the Celtic world, to Scotland, Man, Cornwall and Brittany. If this seems like something of an afterthought, it is certainly not intended to be. The people of these regions must surely have had a mythology every bit as well developed as those of the Irish and the Welsh, no doubt expressed through a storytelling tradition. Unfortunately, these stories do not appear to have been recorded in the early medieval period or, at least, if stories were written down at this time, nothing has survived. This is not to say that no writing at all remains from these places. Early medieval manuscripts certainly do exist, particularly in Scotland but, with the exception of a few marginal notes and scribbles, very little is in the Celtic languages and there are no stories based on the oral tradition.

Where there are no written sources, it is obviously difficult to say very much about the mythology. When stories generated in an oral tradition stop being told, they are lost and cannot be reconstructed. And yet the oral tradition of storytelling, in some of the Celtic regions at least, continued into modern times in folktales. Scholars have tended to be condescending towards such orally transmitted stories – they have a marked preference for written sources, perhaps identifying more with the monastic scribes who recorded the stories in manuscripts than with those who, in the older literature on the subject, are often referred to as 'the illiterate peasantry'.

The stories of the oral tradition can appear unsophisticated to the highly educated members of a literary society, but a balanced and unprejudiced appreciation can uncover multiple layers of meaning and richly developed levels of artistry in these supposedly humble folktales. It is something of an irony that, in more recent times, when academic opinion has been more open to these oral traditions, many of them have declined to the point of extinction. The wider availability of education and subsequent rise in literacy levels can only be seen as good things, but one of the side-effects has been a huge reduction in the occurrence of oral storytelling. These days, we get our stories from books, films, television and the internet, not from the traditional storyteller.

The way we deal with the world around us and how we perceive it has, of course, always been subject to adaptation and change and this is as true of storytelling as it is of anything else. Because of this constant state of change, there is a problem when considering folktales as representatives of a continuous tradition of storytelling that goes back to the mythology-based stories of the pre-Christian world. That problem lies in determining the exact relationship between the folktales and the stories preserved in the early medieval manuscripts. The monastic scribes appear to have been recording stories from the class of professional bards who held positions within the households of the Celtic nobility. The decline of these noble houses, usually the result of pressure of one sort or another from England, put an end to this form of storytelling, but the tradition continued amongst what might be called the common people, particularly where the Celtic languages continued to be widely spoken. The professional bards came from families who had followed the tradition for many generations and the stories and techniques of storytelling were passed down to them through the family. It is easy to assume that, as the Celtic nobility declined, these same families continued their inherited tradition in the reduced circumstances in which they found themselves but it is impossible to know this for certain. If this was indeed the case, then the stories collected in different parts of the Celtic world by folklorists, beginning in the nineteenth century, would represent the survival of a tradition going back many hundreds, possibly even thousands, of years.

The content of folktales is very much up to the individual storyteller, and can be open to all sorts of influences and changing circumstances. The similarity in content and characters between an ancient mythological story and a modern folktale may suggest a relationship which is simply not there. Modern stories of Finn MacCool, for example, may hark back to the warrior hero Fionn mac Cumhaill or may be entirely the inventions of modern authors, borrowing the name in an attempt to invest their stories with a degree of authenticity. With these reservations in mind, the rest of this chapter takes a look at the folktales of the Celtic regions.

Scotland and Man

At its narrowest, the North Channel, the strait between Argyll in the west of Scotland and the north east coast of Northern Ireland, is only twelve miles wide. The connection between the people on either side of this channel, where the Irish Sea meets the Atlantic Ocean, is as obvious now as it must have been over the course of the past few thousand years. Movement between Ireland and Scotland was commonplace and, in the fifth century AD, land on both sides of the channel was united as the kingdom of Dal Riata. Whether this was a result of Irish people moving into Scotland, Scottish people moving into Ireland, or because the people in two regions were so connected as to make the distinction meaningless, is a matter for debate. However, it appears certain that the Celtic language spoken originated in Ireland and spread to Scotland, diverging from the original to form what is now known as Scottish Gaelic.

Christianity also came to Scotland from Ireland. It is traditionally said to have been brought by St Columba, known as Colm Cille in Irish, who founded the monastery on the island of Iona in 563. Illuminated manuscripts were produced here – a case can be made for at least part of *The Book of Kells* being written on Iona – but, by the early ninth century, the exposed position of the monastery made it highly vulnerable to Viking raiders. Valuable items, perhaps including *The Book of Kells*, were moved to the relative safety of monasteries in the Irish Midlands. Anything remaining in Iona at this time would not have survived the Viking raids, which also took a heavy toll of the monks. In 806, everyone at the abbey was found massacred, presumably the victims of the Vikings.

With such close links to Ireland, it is hardly surprising to find echoes of the old Irish stories in the storytelling of the Scottish Gaelic communities of the west coast of Scotland. The survival of such stories among the far-flung, Gaelic-speaking communities of Cape Breton in Nova Scotia has already been mentioned, but examples can also be found closer to home. After the enormous success of the Ossian poems by James Macpherson in the late eighteenth century, and despite their dubious provenance, Celtic folklore became fashionable. A number of folklorists travelled to the west of Scotland to record the actual tales as they existed at the time and were told by Gaelic storytellers.

One of the best of the published collections was John Francis Campbell's *Popular Tales of the West Highlands*, which came out in an edition of four volumes in 1860.[37] The stories related by Campbell came from many different people from all over the Highlands and Hebrides and many were what we might now describe as fairytales, showing influences ranging from Greek mythology to the Brothers Grimm. Others were more recognisably Celtic in origin and included characters from the Irish cycles, particularly Fionn mac Cumhaill. One example is a version of the story of Diarmuid and Gráinne very similar to the story from the Ulster Cycle related in Chapter 3. One of the longest stories, and one of the few to be put together from a number of different sources rather than being told by a single storyteller, is 'The Story of Conall Gulban', a complicated and involved tale of the exploits of a young Irish king. The man-uscripts of Irish pseudo-histories, including *The Book of Invasions*, also tell of Conall Gulban, saying he was one of the eight sons of Niall Noigiallach (Niall of the Nine Hostages), a High King of all Ireland in the late fourth cen-tury. According to these accounts, Conall founded the kingdom of Tír Conaill in what is now County Donegal and was an ancestor of, among many, Colm Cille.

A different strand of folklore relates stories concerning the selkies, seal people who can transform from human beings to seals and back again, allowing them to live both on land and in the water. The English writer David Thomson explored these stories of what he called the seal folk in the Orkneys, Shetland and the west coast of Ireland as well as in the Hebrides, publishing a wonderful book *The People of the Sea* in 1954, relating his travels and the stories he heard.[38] One of the stories, told to him by Margaret Fea while he was on the island of North Ronaldsay in the Orkneys, concerned Brita, the daughter of a laird, described as being tall, fair and possibly of Norwegian her-itage. She set her heart on a man who worked for her father, but was too frightened to tell her father because the man was poor and of lowly birth. After her father died, Brita married the man and was happy for several years. Everything was well between them, except there were no children. Brita began to grow dissatisfied with her husband and, one day, went down to the shore to talk to the selkies. After she cried seven tears into the sea, a selkie put his head above the water to ask her what was wrong. When she explained the problem, he told her to meet him at the same spot at the time of the seven streams, a time relating to one of the two highest tides of the year. She kept the appointment and the selkie came to her in the form of a man. After that first time, she went to the shore to meet the selkie many more times. Later she gave birth to many children, all born with webbed hands and feet, which were clipped by the midwife to separate them and had to be cut regularly to prevent the webs growing back.

Many of the other stories of the selkies tell of sexual relations between seals, both male and female, and people. The selkies transformed themselves into people by shedding their seal skins and the people they were with would often try to make them stay on land by hiding the skins or putting them on themselves. These stories appear to have originated in the Orkneys and could have been influenced by stories from Norway as well as those from the Celtic world. From there they spread along the Scottish and Irish coast and are also known from the Isle of Man, the lump of rock in the Irish Sea, supposedly thrown there by the giant Finn MacCool when he was aiming at a Scottish giant and missed.

Information on the mythology of the Isle of Man is less readily available than for that of Scotland. Its position in the Irish Sea, about equally distant from Ireland, Scotland and the north of England, gives a fair indication of the nature of its stories. The language, now recovering after almost completely dying out in the twentieth century, is related to Irish and Scottish Gaelic and, at one time, it would no doubt have been possible to hear tales of the exploits of Fionn or Finn, or whichever version of the name was in use. An idea of the likely closeness of the mythology to

Ireland and Scotland can actually be found in the very name of the island, said by some to have come from the name of the sea god Manannán mac Lir, although others suggest the land gave its name to the god, not the other way round. Traditionally said to be the first ruler of the people of Man, he is also said to watch over the island to this day.

Cornwall and Brittany

Mythology in Cornwall, to an even greater extent than in Man, has almost entirely been lost. The decline of the language, which became almost entirely extinct in the eighteenth century, occurred before collecting folklore became a fashionable pursuit, leaving the Celtic stories of the region something of a distant memory. In the folklore, a tradition of 'fairy folk' or 'little people' survived, in the form of pixies and buccas (a feature of the other Celtic regions, known as leprechauns in Ireland and knockers in Wales) but these are usually tricksters who interfere with people's lives in the real world and rarely feature in stories. Cornwall is also the setting for many of the Arthurian romances and there are parallels, such as the theme of the love triangle in Tristan and Iseult, between some of these tales and Celtic mythology. However, this could just as easily be a result of each tradition influencing the other as an echo of a distant Celtic past.

The pre-Christian tradition in Cornwall is more apparent in a number of festivals and fairs held in the region, some of which are still much more than just tourist attractions. The parading of the 'Obby 'Oss in Padstow on 1 May can be seen as having roots in the Celtic festival of Beltane, and Morvah Fair, which was held at the beginning of August until it was stopped by the Church establishment in the late nineteenth century because it was seen as encouraging rowdy and drunken behaviour, was synonymous with Lughnasa. The folktale of 'The Giants of Morvah', in which one giant battles with several others over the possession of treasure and the attention of a female giant, ends with a huge wedding feast, the first celebration, so the story says, held on the day that would later become the occasion of the fair. This story could well be a relatively recent one, but some commentators suggest it may have much older roots, possibly even representing the fragmentary survival of a Cornish epic cycle.[39]

The similarities between Cornwall and Brittany go further than the closely related languages, as anyone familiar with the rugged landscapes of the two regions will know. Both are peninsulas jutting out into the Atlantic and, both in terms of the attitudes of the people and in physical distance, they feel remote from the seats of power. Perhaps it is this, together with the perception that they both have cultures under pressure, that has led to a spirit of independence in the two places.

The Breton language has survived to a greater extent than Cornish, despite the efforts to discourage it by the French Government. Folklorists collected a wide range of stories and songs in the nineteenth century, one of the first and best being published as *Barzaz Breiz* (Breton Bards) in the 1830s by Théodore Hersart de la Villemarqué, a French aristocrat with Breton heritage. The most widely known story is 'The Legend of the City of Ys' or, in Breton, *Ker Is*, which literally means 'low city'. The story concerns

Gradlon, the king of the city, and his beautiful golden-haired daughter Dahut, whose mother returned to the sea, from where she came, after Dahut was born. The low-lying city is protected from the sea by a dyke and Dahut is tempted by a stranger she meets, who becomes her lover, to steal the key to the sluice gates in the dyke from the king as he sleeps. Dahut takes the keys and opens the gates. A torrent of water pours in, drowning the city. Gradlon, riding a horse, tries to save his daughter from the flood, but she slips from his grasp and is lost in the water, becoming a mermaid who sings beautiful songs to attract fishermen to her, and to their deaths. Hersart de la Villemarqué's version ends:

As-tu vu, pêcher, la fille de la mer, peignant ses cheveux blondes comme d'or, au soleil de midi, au bord de l'eau?

J'ai vu la blanche fille de la mer, je l'ai même entendre chanter: ses chants étaient plaintefs comme les flots.

(Did you see, fishermen, the girl of the sea, combing her golden blonde hair, in the midday sun by the side of the sea?

I have seen the white girl of the sea, I have listened to her songs, her voice as mournful as the sound of the waves.)[40]

Here, encapsulated in this traditional Breton song first written down in the 1830s, are some of the motifs which recur throughout Celtic mythology: the beautiful fair hair of the goddess, her ability to transform herself, in this case to become a mermaid, and her movement from the land to the sea, from the world of the living to the Otherworld. The story told by the song is a simple one but, just beneath the surface, there are allusions to a way of thinking about the world which comes down to us from the ancestors. Whether we choose to listen to them or not is, of course, entirely another matter.

Notes

1. A summary of developments in the academic discipline of mythology is given in Segal (2004).
2. Taken from the fifth edition of *The Shorter Oxford English Dictionary* (Oxford 2002).
3. This author would, needless to say, be delighted to find this book in a bookshop in whatever section the bookshop staff saw fit to place it.
4. Jackson (1971).
5. The themes touched on here are expanded on in Armstrong (2005).
6. For a discussion of the differences between oral and written cultures, see Ong (1982).
7. Armstrong (2005).
8. *Ibid*
9. Cumbric was a Celtic language related to Welsh and spoken in the north east of England and parts of lowland Scotland. It is thought to have died out in the eleventh century. In recent years attempts have been made to revive it, although the difficulties of pronouncing words in a language which has not been spoken for a thousand years are obvious.
10. James (1999). See also Cunliffe (2001) and Collis (2004) for a discussion on the origins of the idea of

'Celticness'.

11. Julius Caesar's *Commentarii de Bello Gallico* is available in a number of English translations, including *The Gallic War*, translated by Carolyn Hammond (Oxford 1999).

12. Cunliffe (2001).

13. Pryor (2004).

14. Cunliffe (1997).

15. See Sykes (2006) and Oppenheimer (2006) for details of these genetic investigations. Stephen Oppenheimer has given a summary of his findings in the October 2006 issue of Prospect Magazine, available online at www.prospect-magazine.co.uk

16. Oppenheimer (2006).

17. Halpin and Newman (2006).

18. Pryor (2003).

19. Lord (2000), a new edition of a work originally published in 1960.

20. Ong (1982).

21. Philips, Helen, 'Mind Fiction: Why your brain tells tales', *New Scientist,* 7 October 2006.

22. de Burca, Sean (1973). *Aspects of Transmission.* Éigse, 15. As quoted in Nagy, Joseph Falaky (1986), 'Orality in Medieval Irish Narrative: An Overview', *Oral Tradition 12*.

23. Knott and Murphy (1966).

24. Extract from *The Wanderings of Oisin* taken from *The Collected Poems of WB Yeats.* (MacMillan 1950).

25. Cunliffe (2001).

26. Jackson (1964).

27. Gantz (1981).

28. *Ibid.*
29. Ó hÓgáin (2006).
30. MacKillop (2005).
31. Carson (2007).
32. Kinsella (1969).
33. Carson (2007).
34. Kinsella (1969).
35. MacNeil (1987).
36. See entries for Fionn, Fionn File and Fionn mac Cumhaill in Ó hÓgáin (2006).
37. The text of all four volumes of *Popular Tales of the West Highlands* can be found online at www.sacred-texts.com/neu/celt
38. Thomson (new ed. 1996).
39. MacKillop (2005).
40. Taken from de Villemarqué (1923), with my own attempt at a translation.

Bibliography

Texts in English Translation

Gantz, Jeffrey, *Early Irish Myths and Sagas*, Harmondsworth: Penguin Books, 1981

Jackson, Kenneth Hurlstone, *A Celtic Miscellany*, Harmondsworth: Penguin Books, 1971

Koch, John T. and Carey, John (eds), *The Celtic Heroic Age: Literary Sources for Ancient Celtic Europe and Early Ireland and Wales*, 4th edition, Aberystwyth: Celtic Studies Publications, 2003

La Villemarqué, Theodore Hersart, *Barzaz Briez*, Paris: Perrin, new ed. 1923

Mabinogion, The, trans. Jeffrey Gantz, Harmondsworth: Penguin Books, 1976

Mabinogion, The, trans. Sioned Davies, Oxford: OUP, 2007

MacNeil, Joe Neil, *Tales Until Dawn: The World of a Cape Breton Gaelic Story-Teller*, (trans. and ed. John Shaw), Montreal: McGill-Queen's University Press, 1987

Táin, The, trans. Ciaran Carson, Harmondsworth: Penguin Books, 2007

Táin, The, trans. Thomas Kinsella, Oxford: OUP, 1969

Tales of the Elders of Ireland, (trans. Ann Dooley and Harry Roe), Oxford: OUP, 1999

General Books

Armstrong, Karen, *A Short History of Myth*, Edinburgh: Canongate, 2005

Collis, John, *The Celts: Origins, Myths and Inventions,* Stroud: Tempus, 2003

Cunliffe, Barry, *The Ancient Celts*, Oxford: OUP, 1997

Cunliffe, Barry, *Facing the Ocean: The Atlantic and its Peoples 8000BC – AD 1500*, Oxford: OUP, 2001

Green, Miranda J., *Dictionary of Celtic Myth and Legend*, London: Thames and Hudson, 1997

Halpin, Andy and Newman, Conor, *Ireland: An Oxford Archaeological Guide to Sites from the Earliest Times to AD 1600*, Oxford: OUP, 2006

Jackson, Kenneth Hurlstone, *The Oldest Irish Tradition: A Window on the Iron Age*, Cambridge: CUP, 1964

James, Simon, *The Atlantic Celts: Ancient People or Modern Invention?*, London: British Museum Press, 1999

Knott, Elenor and Murphy, Gerard, *Early Irish Literature*, London: Routledge, 1966

Lord, Albert B., *The Singer of Tales*, Harvard: Harvard University Press, new ed. 2000

MacKillop, James, *Myths and Legends of the Celts*, Harmondsworth: Penguin Books, 2005

Ó hÓgáin, Dáithí, *The Lore of Ireland: An Encyclopaedia of Myth, Legend and Romance*, Cork: The Collins Press, 2006

Ó hÓgáin, Dáithí, *The Sacred Isle: Belief and Religion in Pre-Christian Ireland*, Cork: The Collins Press, 1999

Ong, Walter J., *Orality and Literacy: The Technologizing of the Word*, London: Methuen, 1982

Oppenheimer, Stephen, *The Origins of the British*, London: Robinson, 2006

Pryor, Francis, *Britain AD; A Quest for Arthur, England and the Anglo-Saxons*, London: HarperCollins, 2004

Pryor, Francis, *Britain BC: Life in Britain and Ireland Before the Romans*, London: HarperCollins, 2003

Segal, David, *Myth: A Very Short Introduction*, Oxford: OUP, 2004

Sykes, Bryan, *Blood of the Isles: Exploring the Genetic Roots of Our Tribal History*, London: Bantam Press, 2006

Thomson, David, *The People of the Sea: Celtic Tales of the Seal-Folk*, Edinburgh: Canongate, new ed. 1996

Index